Illustrating fashion

Kathryn McKelvey
&
Janine Munslow

Blackwell
Publishing

© 1997 by Blackwell Science Ltd
a Blackwell Publishing company

Editorial offices:
Blackwell Publishing Ltd, 9600 Garsington Road, Oxford OX4 2DQ, UK
    Tel: +44 (0) 1865 776868
Blackwell Publishing Inc., 350 Main Street, Malden, MA 02148-5020, USA
    Tel: +1 781 388 8250
Blackwell Publishing Asia Pty Ltd, 550 Swanston Street, Carlton, Victoria 3053, Australia
    Tel: +61 (0)3 8359 1011

First published 1997
Reprinted 1999, 2000, 2003, 2004, 2005

ISBN 10: 0-632-04024-6
ISBN 13: 978-0-632-04024-7

Library of Congress Cataloging-in-Publication Data is available

A catalogue record for this title is available from the British Library

Set in 9.5/11 pt Palatino
by SNP Best-set Typesetter Ltd, Hong Kong
Printed and bound by Replika Press Pvt. Ltd, India

The publisher's policy is to use permanent paper from mills that operate a sustainable forestry policy, and which has been manufactured from pulp processed using acid-free and elementary chlorine-free practices. Furthermore, the publisher ensures that the text paper and cover board used have met acceptable environmental accreditation standards.

For further information on Blackwell Publishing, visit our website:
www.blackwellpublishing.com

CONTENTS

ACKNOWLEDGEMENTS

We would like to thank the publisher, Richard Miles, for giving us the opportunity to produce this book. Also, the Department of Design at the University of Northumbria and particularly the staff on the Fashion Marketing Route for giving us their encouragement and full support.

We would also like to thank the professional contributors, Desmonds Childrenswear Division, International Design Exchange Limited (IN.D.EX.), Milou Ket Styling and Design, Newcastle Fashion Centre – Sally Craig and Fiona Raeside, Guerrilla Farm, Helen Pocock, Helen Farnell, Steven Tulip, Janice Chadfield, Chantelle Cockle, Chris Hogg, Lisa Bratley, Janet Hart and Jacqui Lee.

On a personal note I would like to thank my husband, Ian, for his patience and common sense, and my parents and Ian's for helping to look after Emily and Lucy whilst I was knee deep in drawings and text.

Kathryn McKelvey

I would like to thank my parents, husband, Neil, and boys, Benjamin and Laurence.

Janine Munslow

INTRODUCTION

Fashion illustration is a form of stylised drawing; it seeks to communicate not only an artistic representation, but a sense of style. Illustrators need to be draughtsmen, able to draw in a variety of ways with a strong awareness of the vagaries of fashion. These skills must then be applied to the commercial world where visual communication is essential in the process of developing and selling ideas. The techniques in this book will help you to foster the necessary skills and provide the background knowledge of their applications within the fashion industry.

This book is intended to be used by anyone wishing to study fashion illustration or design. An ability or some experience of drawing is always an advantage but it is in no way imperative. The first part of the book will help you to develop and experiment with basic drawing skills through drawing exercises and media techniques. The second half of the book provides an introduction to contemporary fashion illustration.

Illustration plays a significant part in the manufacturing and marketing of fashion clothing and accessories. The fashion business operates through a network of organisations, each having its own function. Many different companies may deal with one garment before it eventually finds its home in the customer's wardrobe. At each stage the companies involved need to categorise the product visually and describe it, either as part of the production or the marketing process. This creates a need for different types of drawing and for special illustrative skills.

The illustrator's traditional work of portraying fashionable styles in magazines and newspapers has been superseded by photography during the second half of the 20th century. Illustration is now more hidden from public view but is still used extensively in the commercial development of a garment or product. The information contained in this book reflects on the role of illustration in the fashion industry today, and will help you to understand the work of the illustrator by providing an introduction to:

> The recent history of fashion illustration
> Drawing and media techniques
> Fabric representation
> Developing and communicating visual concepts
> Illustrating and promoting new styles
> Drawing for manufacture, by creating 'blue prints' and specifications
> Areas of specialism.

New technology and the use of computer aided design and graphics have had considerable impact on the work of illustrators and designers. The possibilities of information technology and its use for visual communication are vast. Of course there are areas of design and illustration where technology is at the forefront of scientific development, but in this book we aim to give a more general picture of its application in the workplace. Some of the examples provided from the industry are executed with expensive equipment or software; however, other exercises and examples (the Claris Works on Apple Macintosh Performa illustrations) are relatively simple to perform and this type of equipment is much more accessible to the individual or student.

Computer programs allow the illustrator to create accurate technical drawings which in turn can be flood filled with any pattern, texture or colour, saving the most time consuming work of 'colouring up' the same design in different colourways and fabrications. Many designers now use computer programs to illustrate their collections, scanning in their original art work and then applying colourways and fabrication. Technology, however, is only an aid to the creative process and not a substitute for the manual skills the illustrator needs to learn from experience and practice.

The content and structure of this book reflects the new role of illustration in today's fashion industry.

How to use this book

If you have drawing experience:

Even if you have abundant drawing experience it is still most valuable to experiment with media and drawing exercises. See *Drawing from Life – Drawing exercises* and *Media Techniques*. Some people will have disproportionate skills: an excellent draughtsman, perhaps, but without a developed sense of fashion awareness. See *Fashion Illustration* and *Sketch Books*.

If you have little drawing experience:

Don't despair! It is quite possible to become a competent illustrator, particularly if you have fashion awareness. The perceptive skills needed to draw well are the same as required to judge proportion, balance, colour, etc. See *Historical Perspective, Drawing from Life – Drawing exercises, Media Techniques* and *Fabric Representation*.

Beginning to illustrate:

NB: This information assumes the bulk of the design/collection has been completed using working drawings in your sketch book and that you are trying to promote and present the designs. If you have not started designing refer to *Sketch Books – Design development, Fashion Illustration* and *Drawing for Manufacture* for help in putting your initial ideas down on paper.

(1) Decide what you are trying to achieve. Look at the section on *Fashion Illustration* or *Drawing for Manufacture* to choose the correct method of presenting your work. What is your market? Refer to *Specialist Areas* if you are designing for maternity, active sportswear, lingerie, swimwear, or accessories. What does the 'look' consist of? Refer to the *Historical Perspective* and section on *Fashion Illustration* for help in defining a style if you are having problems 'seeing' your designs presented.

(2) Draw figures lightly in pencil; reference should be made to the poses offered or to your own life class. Choose a model that is close to the 'look' you require and is posed in a way that would help to suggest the market level. For example, if you are designing a womenswear collection for the young that is very fashionable, then choose a young model with the right appearance of 'attitude' and liveliness. Go to *Drawing from Life* – see the various sections on poses and heads, hands and feet.

(3) Sketch the designs onto the figures with accessories to complete the total look, using a light box.

(4) Refer to *Media Techniques* to decide what effect you are going to use to illustrate your designs. For example, if you are illustrating a collection using predominantly white fabrics, then perhaps you should consider using a technique where the background is dark and white media are applied to it.

(5) Refer to *Fabric Representation* to render the fabrics used in designing.

(6) Go to the *Drawing for Manufacture* section to render any working drawings as part of your presentation.

(7)   If a promotional illustration of a particular garment is required then refer to *Fashion Illustration – Drawing for promotion* and back to *Sketch Books* for reference to any 'thematic' information that may be useful for the presentation; see, for example, *Specialist Areas – Swimwear/Lingerie*.

HISTORICAL PERSPECTIVE

The following is a brief history of fashion illustration from before the First World War to the 1990s.

This exercise is very much simplified for the purposes of investigating line and proportion in fashion illustration in the 20th century. Each montage has a list of general points about the development of fashion illustration.

It is hoped that a feeling for each decade will be provided by being as broad in approach as possible. Nevertheless, trends do not always fit tidily into decades but are transitional.

1910s

Fashion illustrations were inspired by Art Nouveau (natural, curving forms reflecting the decorative art of the time) and exotic influences such as the 'Oriental' influence derived from the theatre, Tyrolean influences and the Ballet Russe. The illustrations were quite realistic in treatment and proportion.

1920s

The drawing style became more simplified, angular and linear, in keeping with the silhouette. The figure was exaggerated to look longer and leaner. The illustrations had a two-dimensional quality. Compositions were influenced by the modern art movement. Drawings were slick and glossy reflecting an interest in glamour.

1930s

Fashion returned to a curved, more feminine silhouette. The actual drawing line became softer, curvier and textural. Drawings were expertly executed in what was the start of the golden age of fashion illustration. Proportion returned to a more realistic interpretation. Illustrative styles were influenced by art movements like Surrealism.

1940s

Fashion illustration was very much a continuation of what emerged in the 1930s. The early part of the decade was an age of brilliant draughtsmanship and illustration reached its zenith. After the Second World War illustration became more romantic in expression.

1950s

Fashion illustration continued to be of a high standard. Illustrators met challenges in representing the new synthetic fabric developments. Illustrations were highly stylised reflecting the aspirations of consumers desperate for glamour.

1960s

The style of fashion illustration from the 1950s continued into the early 1960s but was ultimately usurped by a more modern look. Poses altered, indicating a new freedom for women. The fashion model had a new, younger look, because of the emergence of the 'teenager' in the late fifties. The typical pose changed from demure to more dynamic and dramatic, with a witty, optimistic aspect, expressing hedonism. Photography became very fashionable and illustration declined in popularity. Photographers became celebrities in their own right.

1970s

Fashion illustration became marginalised as photography continued to be fashionable. Initially the style of illustration was influenced by decorative art styles developing in the 1960s, such as Pop Art and Psychedelia. The latter half of the 1970s saw highly finished realism emerging.

1980s

The fashion industry expanded from the progression of the 1960s and market forces demanded more forward thinking information. This could not be provided by photography so a new role for illustration followed. Magazines reverted to featuring small amounts of fashion illustration. Illustrators' work was innovative and experimental.

1990s and beyond

Fashion illustration has an important communicative role within the fashion industry but remains generally unpopular within press and editorial. Photography still remains popular and information technology has extended its possibilities. However, there are fashion cycles and draughtsmanship in magazines communicating with the public could become popular again as we move into the next millennium.

Drawing from life model, courtesy of Naomi Austin.

DRAWING FROM LIFE

Perception and observation

How we see an object is determined by what we are looking for. A garment will be viewed very differently by a designer, or photographer, or wearer.

Illustration is a process of selection, what is chosen to be drawn and what is not. Every person holds a unique perspective of reality. A successful or pleasing fashion illustration selects only what is necessary to create a drawing which reflects a particular fashion statement. Key elements are exaggerated; unnecessary items are rejected.

A representational drawing of the figure accurately records line, form, detail and proportion. Fashion illustration by its nature selects and rejects information, stylising the image.

When drawing a figure, looking at form is important. Many drawings are preconceived ideas of what exists, rather than what is really there. Learning to 'see' is a fundamental part of drawing. Observational skills and the ability to record visual information accurately can be developed by continued practice.

It may be easier when beginning to analyse figures to regard them as a series of blocks and cylinders and to disregard distracting detail, such as folds, creases, facial features, etc. Build the figure first in masses, and then within each of these masses form the varying planes which represent the body.

Drawing

The quality of the line needed to suggest a gesture, movement or pose is important. The line created is linked to the movement of the artist's shoulder, elbow, wrist and fingers through to pencil, crayon or brush. Variations of movement can change the line from a sweep to a spidery crawl. All artists have their own individual 'handwriting'.

Drawings which leave the viewer's mind to 'finish' have an appealing freshness and vigour. Overworked drawings can appear flat and uninteresting.

Much of what makes a good illustration relates to what is left out rather than included. Many artists' rough sketches are better, fresher and more immediate than a more 'finished' work. Rough sketches can be less self-conscious, more simple and direct. Knowing when a drawing is 'finished' is subjective and only learned from experience.

Drawing and observing the human form is a huge subject and can only be explored in a restricted manner in this book. It is important to stress that there is no real substitute to drawing from life and the experience that this intense type of study brings. Drawing and looking often will help to build up a store of visual knowledge enabling you to create illustrations from memory.

Keep a sketch book, draw friends or people in the street, standing and in motion. Swimming pools, dance classes, etc. are ideal locations, or draw yourself in a full length mirror. See the section on *Sketch Books*.

Stop and reconsider your drawing frequently.

Look at your drawing in a mirror – this will give you a chance to reassess your work.

Figure construction

Figures can be defined in terms of masses and planes. It can be easier to think of the body in terms of boxes and cylinders, from the head to the fingers.

The hip tilts down on the leg which is not carrying the body weight.

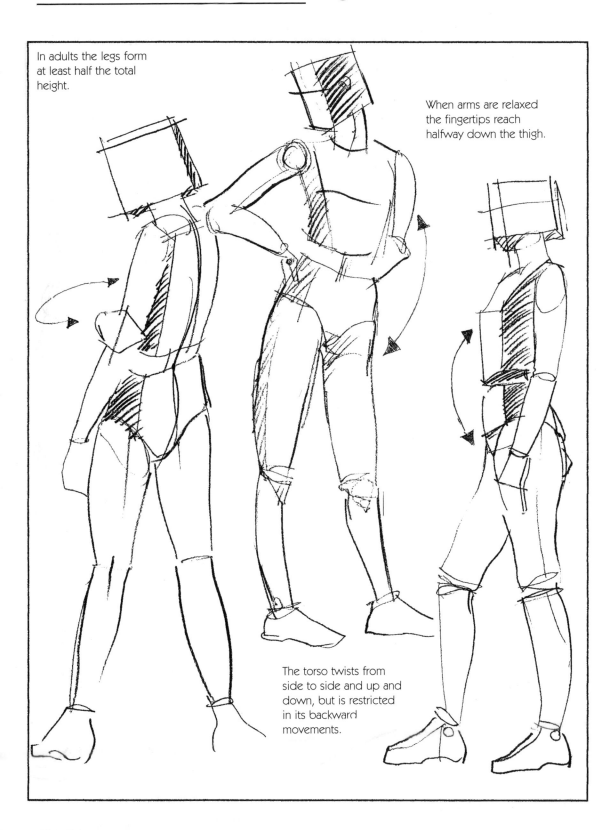

In adults the legs form at least half the total height.

When arms are relaxed the fingertips reach halfway down the thigh.

The torso twists from side to side and up and down, but is restricted in its backward movements.

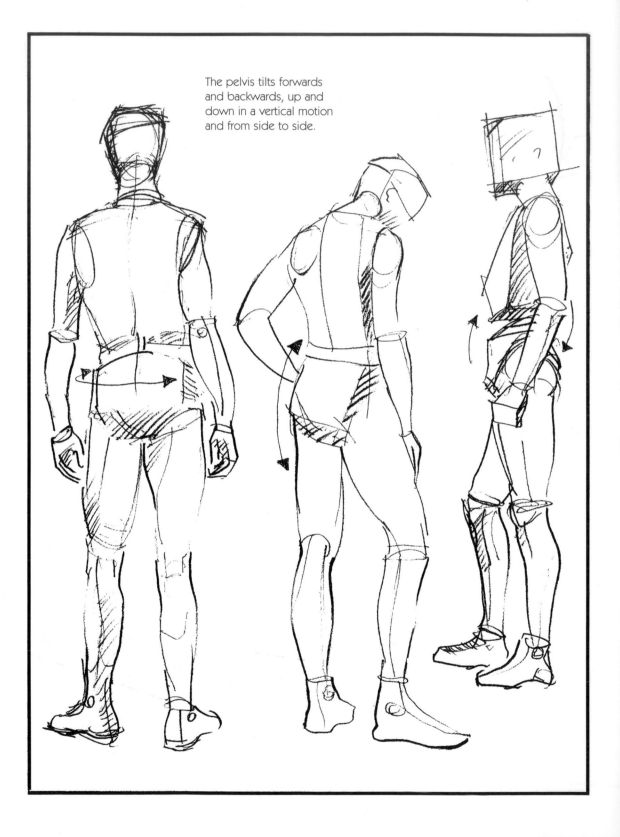

The pelvis tilts forwards and backwards, up and down in a vertical motion and from side to side.

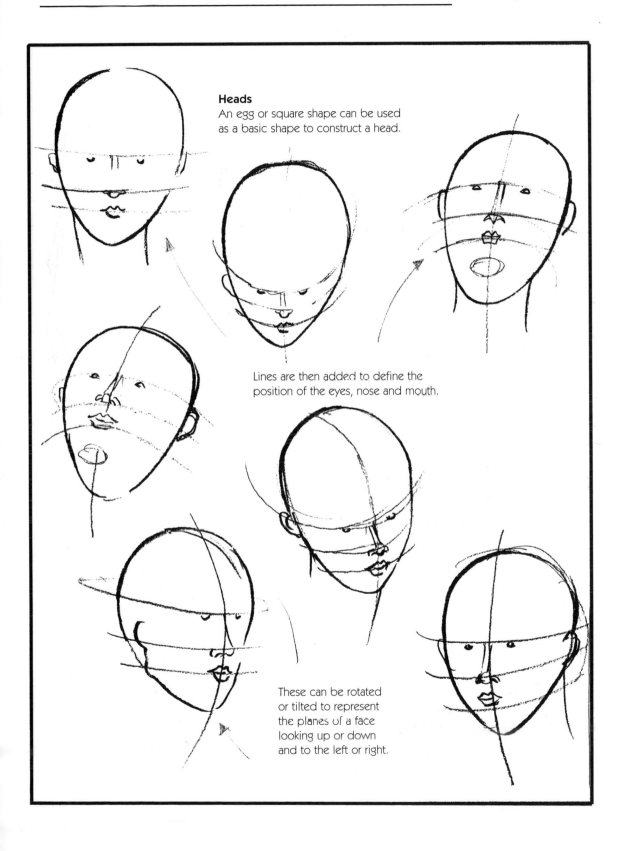

Heads
An egg or square shape can be used as a basic shape to construct a head.

Lines are then added to define the position of the eyes, nose and mouth.

These can be rotated or tilted to represent the planes of a face looking up or down and to the left or right.

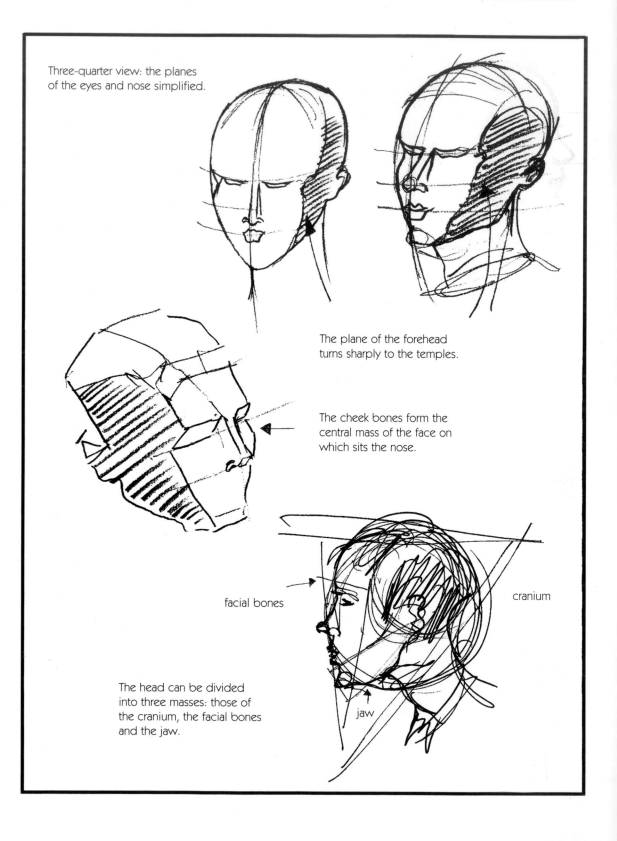

Three-quarter view: the planes
of the eyes and nose simplified.

The plane of the forehead
turns sharply to the temples.

The cheek bones form the
central mass of the face on
which sits the nose.

facial bones

cranium

jaw

The head can be divided
into three masses: those of
the cranium, the facial bones
and the jaw.

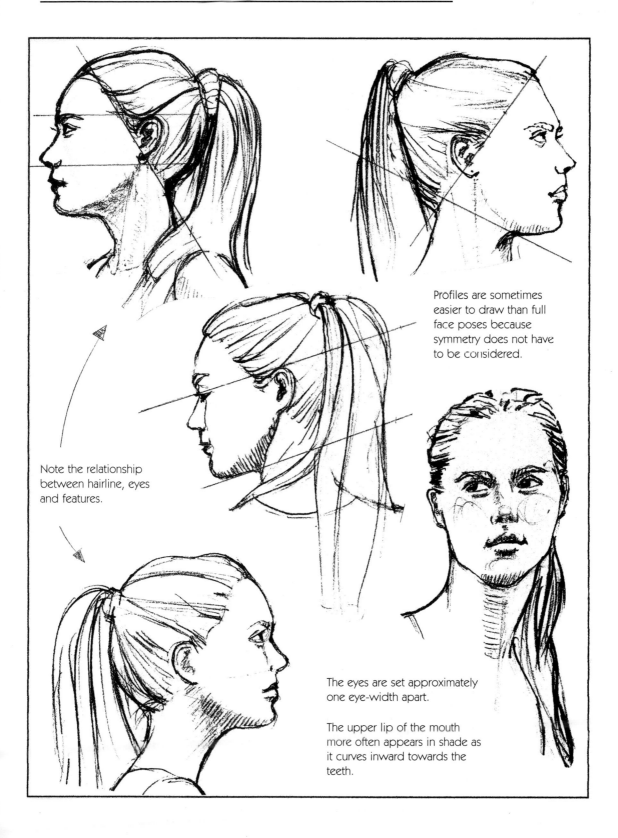

Profiles are sometimes
easier to draw than full
face poses because
symmetry does not have
to be considered.

Note the relationship
between hairline, eyes
and features.

The eyes are set approximately
one eye-width apart.

The upper lip of the mouth
more often appears in shade as
it curves inward towards the
teeth.

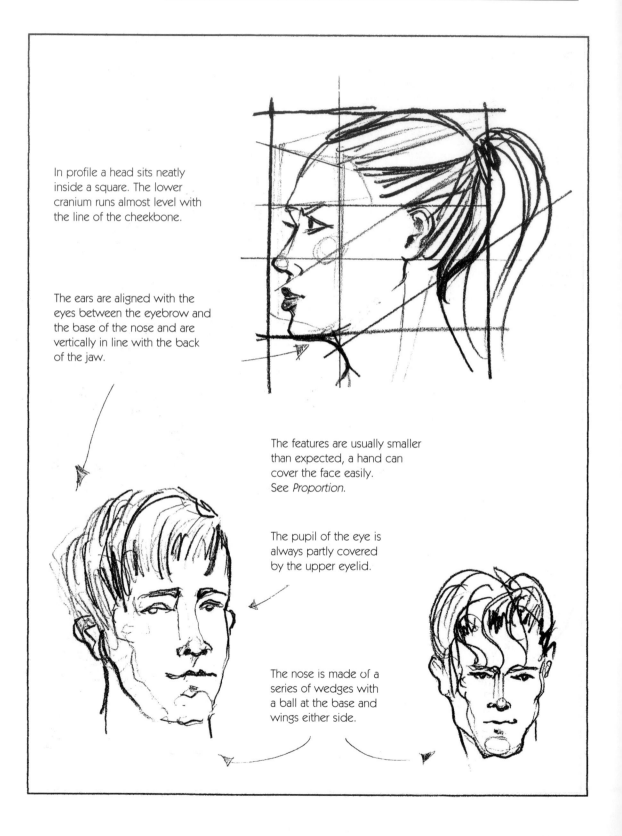

In profile a head sits neatly inside a square. The lower cranium runs almost level with the line of the cheekbone.

The ears are aligned with the eyes between the eyebrow and the base of the nose and are vertically in line with the back of the jaw.

The features are usually smaller than expected, a hand can cover the face easily.
See *Proportion*.

The pupil of the eye is always partly covered by the upper eyelid.

The nose is made of a series of wedges with a ball at the base and wings either side.

Drawing clothes

To draw clothes convincingly you must be aware of the body within; garments are cut or draped on the body. Many of the folds created by movement and tension are predictable. Obviously the type of fabric used will display its own intrinsic behaviour. See *Fabric Representation*.

The knee, thigh and elbow produce most tension and resulting creases. Where the torso twists and bends tension and folding is also evident; this is often what gives the pose dynamism. Another way of suggesting the figure is to use the pattern or texture of the garment and its resulting distortions. Stripes, for example, are very useful for expressing the hidden form.

Fabrics which are stiff, such as denim, create deep creases and impressions where the limbs flex.

Creases are created, particularly in tailored garments, where tension occurs due to movement.

Balance

In order for figures to appear balanced and the poses true to life, it is important to understand the centre of balance and how the weight of the body is usually distributed on one or both legs.

The balance runs through the neck and generally to the leg on which the weight is placed. In most relaxed standing positions the head remains above the foot which is supporting the weight.

Drawing exercises

Experiment with line quality i.e. drawing lines fast and slow – sensitivity.

Communicate information using line only – no symbols e.g. joy, fear, excitement, anger.

Large scale – draw life size and even larger!

Small scale – draw two inches high and smaller!

Self portrait, time limit of half an hour.

Interchange media e.g. ink, pastels, coloured pencils.

Line drawing – use line only.

Tone only – no line.

Negative space – draw silhouette only, look around the subject.

Draw from many perspectives – foreshorten.

Draw from below and look up; draw from above and look down.

Draw without using an eraser.

Direct observation – trace the line of subject by looking at it and not the paper.

Deliberately use line thickness to indicate distance or perspective.

Draw with non-preferred hand.

Draw without taking media off page.

Analyse and draw apparent shapes only.

Draw using geometric shapes only.

Draw using colour blocking.

Trace a reasonable drawing with rapidograph and light box – altering as required.

Use colour to create depth – stronger colour at the front, paler colour receding – try collage as well as other media.

Look at the subject and then turn away, record.

Copy two dimensional images upside down – so that the image looks unfamiliar.
If a slide projector is accessible use it to superimpose images/patterns on models or

even project an image on a wall and trace as large scale.

Style models/friends in different mixes of clothing and draw.

Do a partial drawing and move onto someone else's (if working with others).

Ask for permission to draw children at school in a variety of activities – gestural drawing!

Emulate artists and the media they have used – try something similar but try to achieve quicker results.

Observe the figure – static and posed, in movement (in dance/keep fit classes, swimming pools or on the street), shopping, in cafes or restaurants.

Observe and draw the figure in long poses – three hours.

Observe and draw the figure in very short poses – one minute.

Draw objects in museums and galleries.

Draw the figure from foot to head!

Proportion

The linear subdivisions of objects and shapes (buildings, a facade, garment or painting, etc.) can 'feel' either right or wrong. A sense of proportion is inherent in the experience of perception. What seems right or wrong, unbalanced or in harmony will change in accordance with cultural and historical perspectives, for example, the proportional differences between womenswear illustrations before the First World War and after. See *Historical Perspective*.

Since proportion deals with relativity there must be a unit of measurement; this is usually the head. It is useful when discussing the length of figures for fashion drawing to relate to the proportion in these terms.

Ordinarily adult figures range between seven to eight heads in length. Illustrators have elongated this form from eight to more than fifteen heads according to the dictates of time and fashion.

Figures that are overly exaggerated tend to have extra length in the legs. Occasionally different body areas are exaggerated or reduced in order to promote current trends. Neo-Classical fashion plates, for example, show the hands and feet proportionately smaller than is realistic. In contrast, illustrations from the late 1980s show over-exaggerated feet.

The waist, in the adult figure, is generally positioned at approximately $2\frac{1}{2}$ heads, the hips are at $3\frac{1}{2}$ heads, the knees at $5\frac{1}{2}$. These guidelines are a generalisation and can vary due to fashion trends. Refer to Figures A, B and C.

Children's proportions are not elongated because this would change the apparent age of the child. Their proportion is naturally exaggerated within the body length, for example babies' heads are large in comparison to their body ($3\frac{1}{2}$ to 4 heads in length) and they have to be drawn as an apparent exaggeration. Their features are generally enhanced. Refer to Figure D.

Colour and contrast can effect the perceived proportion of a drawing; this can be used dramatically in illustration.

The printing confines of this book only allow the use of black, white and tone. Therefore composition, contrast and proportion have been important considerations.

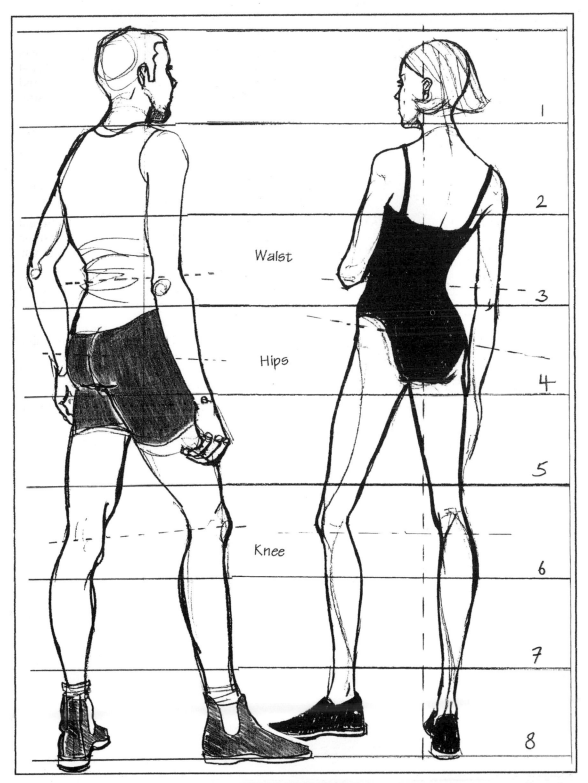

Waist

Hips

Knee

1
2
3
4
5
6
7
8

Natural proportions

Figure A

proportion – elongated figures

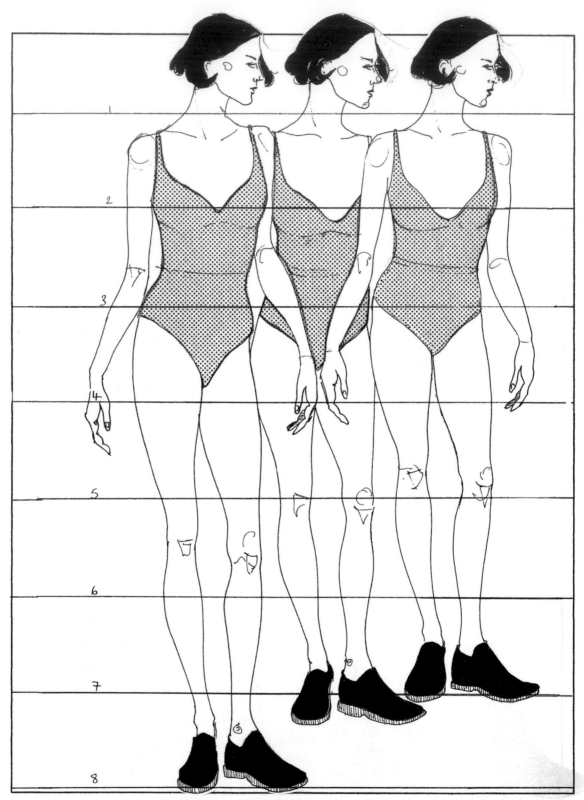

Comparison of proportionately elongated figures

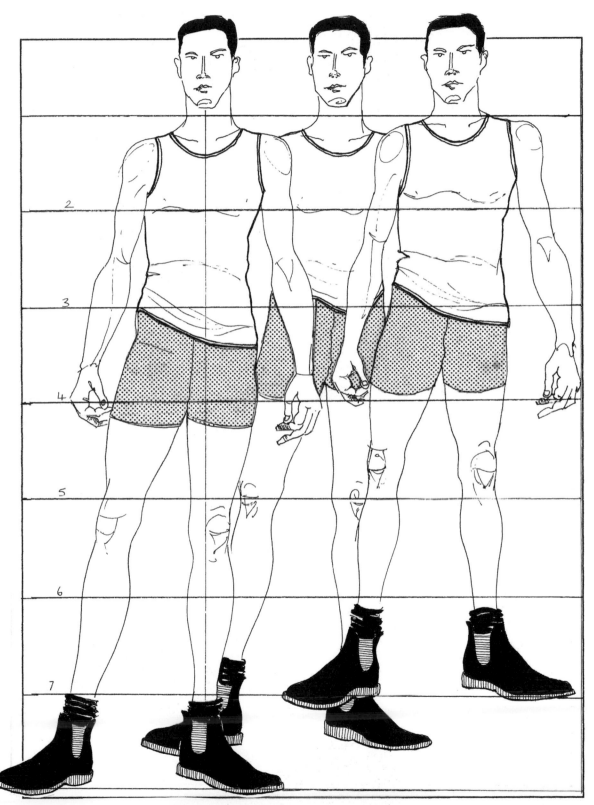

Comparison of proportionately elongated figures   Figure C

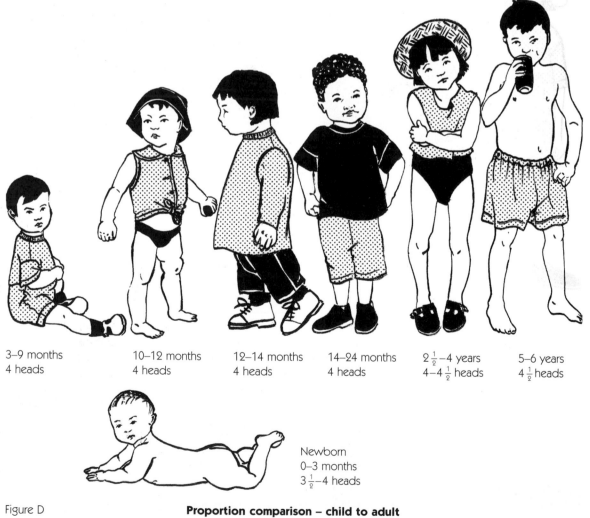

3–9 months
4 heads

10–12 months
4 heads

12–14 months
4 heads

14–24 months
4 heads

$2\frac{1}{2}$–4 years
4–$4\frac{1}{2}$ heads

5–6 years
$4\frac{1}{2}$ heads

Newborn
0–3 months
$3\frac{1}{2}$–4 heads

Figure D   **Proportion comparison – child to adult**

| 7–9 years | 10–11 years | 12–14 years | adult female | adult male |
| 5 heads | $5\frac{1}{2}$ heads | 6 heads | $7\frac{1}{2}$ heads | $7\frac{1}{2}$ heads |

women's poses

The following pages contain women's, men's and children's poses intended as a starting point for your work.

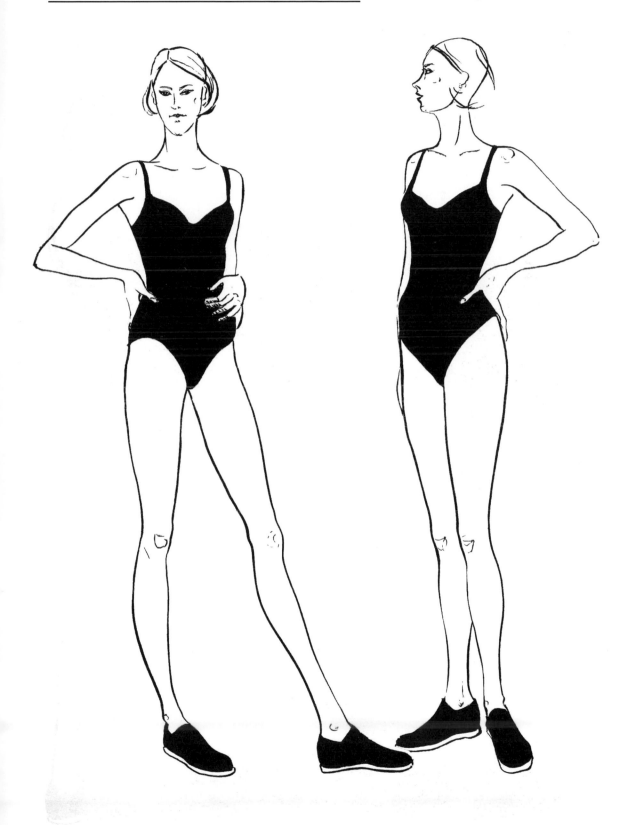

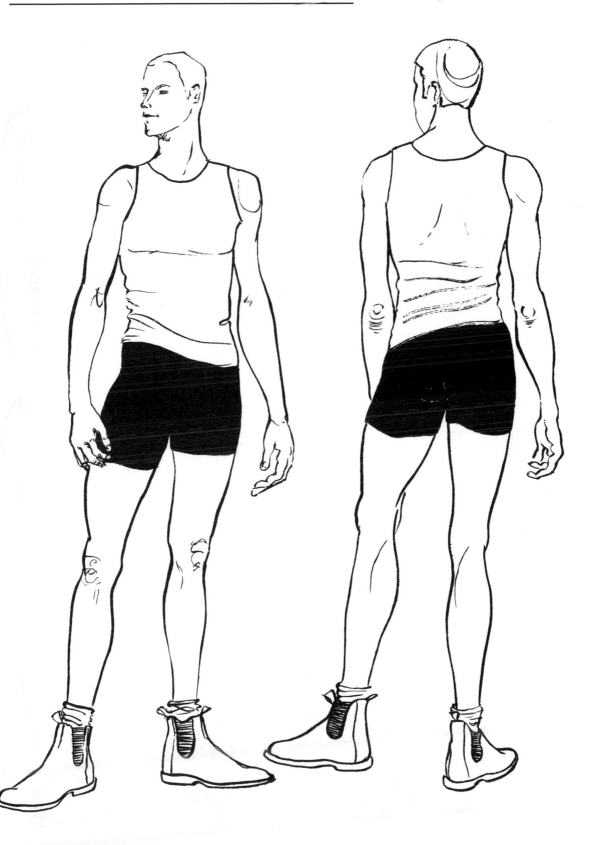

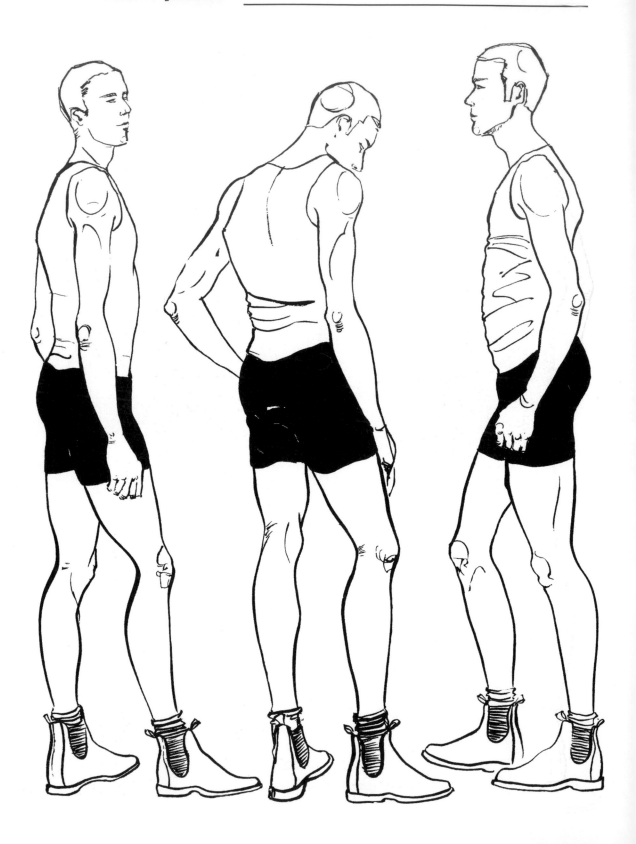

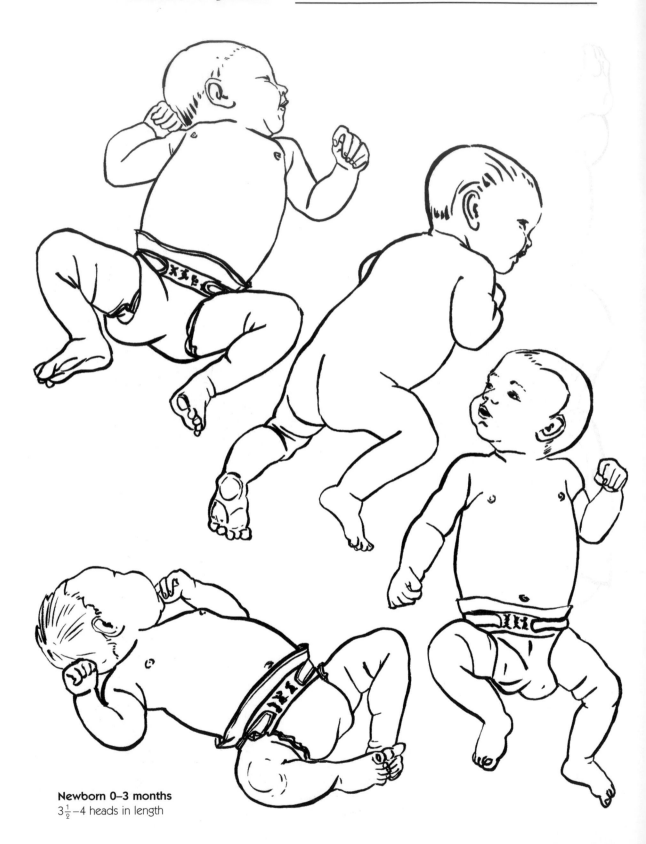

Newborn 0–3 months
$3\frac{1}{2}$–4 heads in length

3–9 months
4 heads in length

9–12 months
4 heads in height

12–18 months
4 heads in height

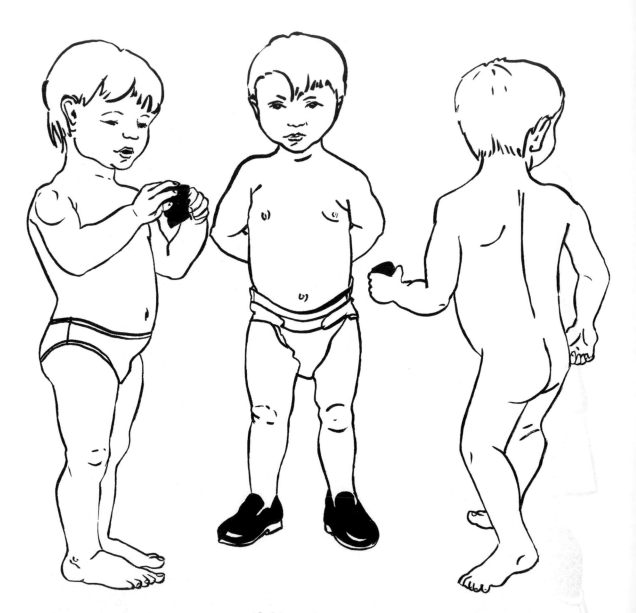

18–24 months
4 heads in height

2–2½ years
4 heads in height

2–2$\frac{1}{2}$ years
4 heads in height

2½–3 years

3–4 years
$4\frac{1}{2}$ heads in height

4–5 years
$4\frac{1}{2}$ heads in height

6–8 years
5 heads in height

6–8 years
5 heads in height

9–11 years
$5\frac{1}{2}$ heads in height

12–14 years
6 heads in height

Constructing a face – woman

1. Choose a photograph or attend a life class. Draw an egg shape/oval after observing the subject, complete with neck – look at the angle of the neck.
2. Divide the oval into two halves. Look at the nose and mouth and draw a line from top to bottom of the oval that will be the centre of the nose and mouth position. This depends upon the angle of the face and the direction in which it is pointing.
3. Dissect the other line equally on either side with the width of an eye, then indicate the eye positions on this line.
4. Observe the bottom half of the oval and halve it again from side to side – this will indicate the base of the nose. Roughly divide in two the bottom quarter for the mouth position. Double check all construction lines with reference to the subject.
5. Lightly draw in the line of the hair using all of the previous construction lines as a guide.
6. Start to draw the detail of the eyes in the positions previously indicated.
7. Draw in the details of the nose and ear – always referring to and double checking construction lines and the subject.
8. Draw in the details of the mouth using the previously plotted construction line.
9. Add any details, such as the hair. Refine the shaping of the jaw, referring to the subject, and add any shadows or highlights. Erase all pencil guidelines.

Three-quarter view with sunglasses – man

1. Choose a photograph or attend a life class. Draw an egg shape or oval after observing the subject. Look at the angle or tilt of the head and record the oval accordingly.
2. Divide the oval into two halves. Look at the nose and mouth and draw a line from top to bottom of the oval. This will indicate the position of the nose and mouth and, subsequently, the eyes. This particular example is a three-quarter view of the head where more of one side of the face is seen than the other. Therefore the guideline is indicated toward the right of the face.
3. Working with the guideline half way down the head, plot the position of the eyes. There will not be an equal eye width between the eyes.
4. Working with the lower half of the oval, divide it again to plot the base of the nose. Roughly divide the bottom quarter for the mouth position. Double check all construction lines with reference to the subject.
5. Lightly draw in the line of the hair using all of the previous construction lines as a guide.
6. Draw in the sunglasses, using the previous guidelines for the eyes.
7. Draw in the details of the nose and ear – always referring to and double checking construction lines and the subject.
8. Draw in the details of the mouth using the previously plotted guidelines.
9. Add any details, such as the hair and the reflective light in the sunglasses. Correct the shape of the jaw, referring to the subject, and add any highlights or shadows. Erase all pencil guidelines.

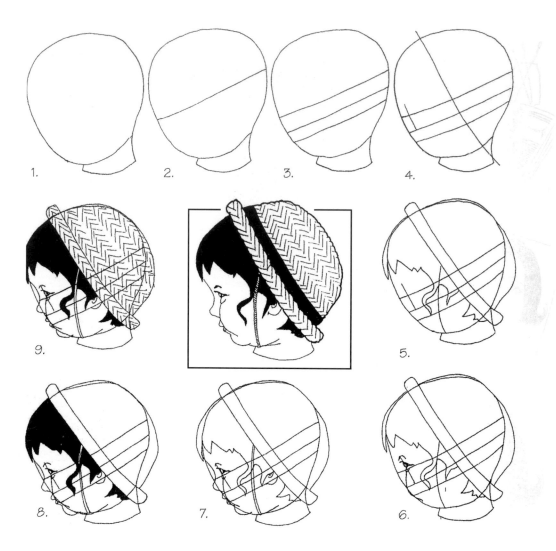

Profile with hat – child

1. Choose a photograph or draw children at play. Draw an oval and neck shape with reference to the subject. This is a profile of the head and is broader in appearance than a frontal view of the head.
2. Divide the oval in two with reference to the top of the ear, allow this to direct the line.
3. Divide the bottom half of the oval in two with a line that runs parallel to the first. Divide the upper section of this half with another parallel line.
4. Plot the position of the eye with reference to the subject. Mark the angle of the brim of the hat with reference to the other guidelines.
5. Draw the shape of the hat and the hairline.
6. Draw in the eye and cheek with reference to the subject.
7. Draw in the nose, mouth and ear.
8. Render the hair.
9. Render the detail of the hat. Erase all pencil guidelines.

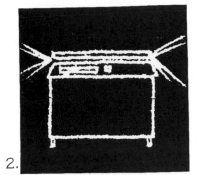

Developing heads from found imagery

1. Choose a photographic image of a face that has strong contrast (shadows).
2. Photocopy.
3. Pick out the dark areas, in pencil, on a light box or against a window.
4. Reduce the image to the appropriate size on a photocopier.
5.&6. The image may now be traced off, enhanced or cut out and pasted directly on the illustration.
7. Observing and sketching faces is a good way of improving drawing techniques.
8.&9. Drawing different hair styles is also helpful.

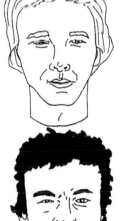

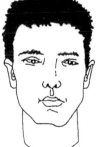

babies' and toddlers' heads

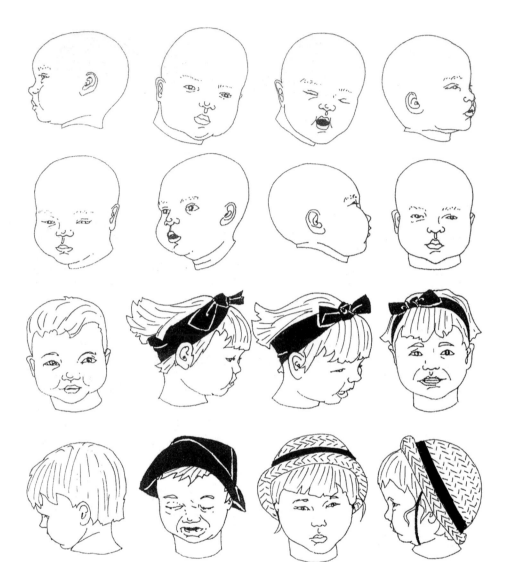

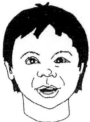

proportion – heads, hands and feet _____

The head is used as the unit of measurement.

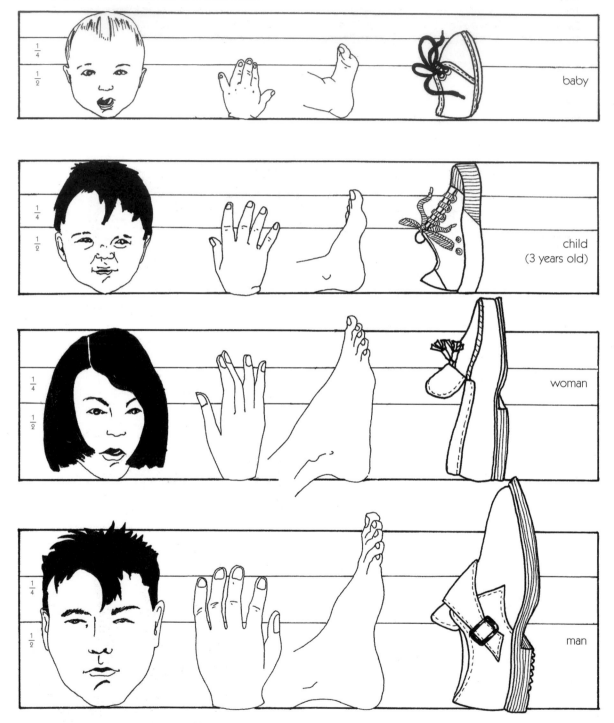

$\frac{1}{4}$
$\frac{1}{2}$
baby

$\frac{1}{4}$
$\frac{1}{2}$
child
(3 years old)

$\frac{1}{4}$
$\frac{1}{2}$
woman

$\frac{1}{4}$
$\frac{1}{2}$
man

Proportion – heads, hands, feet and footwear

Proportion

The length of the hand and wrist is two thirds of a forearm. Index and middle fingers are about the same length.
Each finger has three segments and the thumb two.
The combined length of the last two bones of the fingers is equal to the first.

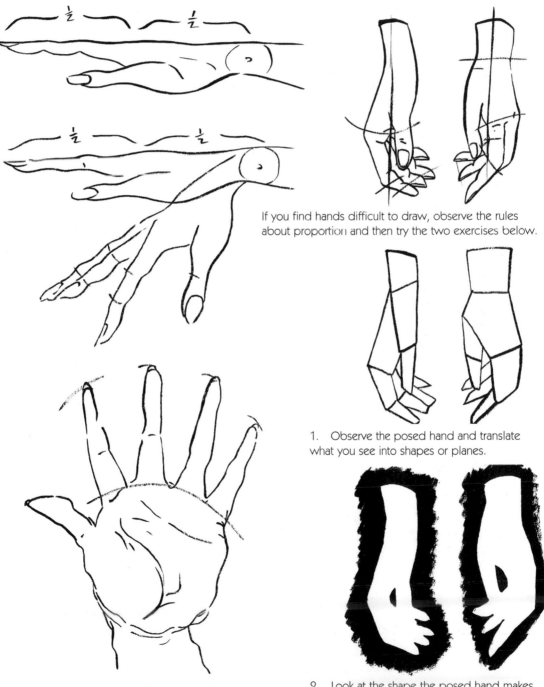

If you find hands difficult to draw, observe the rules about proportion and then try the two exercises below.

1.   Observe the posed hand and translate what you see into shapes or planes.

2.   Look at the shape the posed hand makes in space and draw the silhouette only.

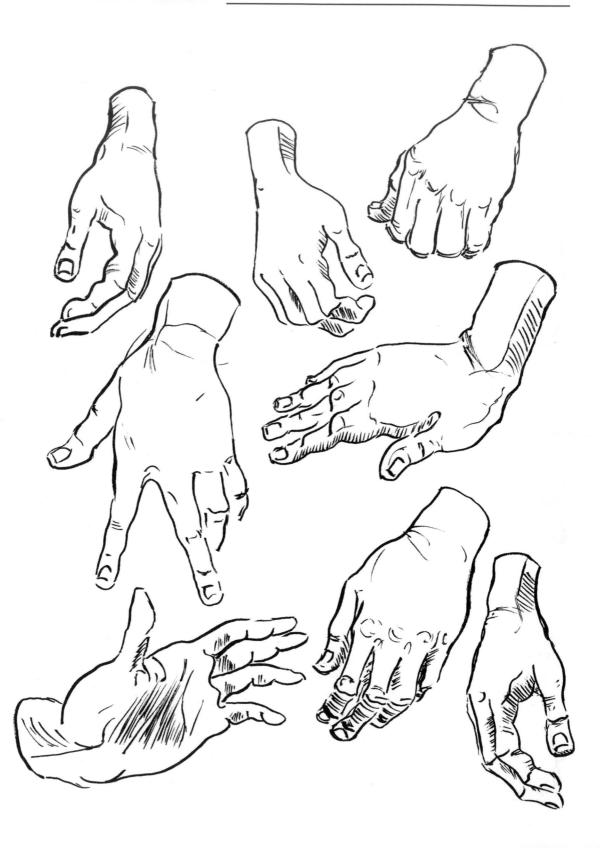

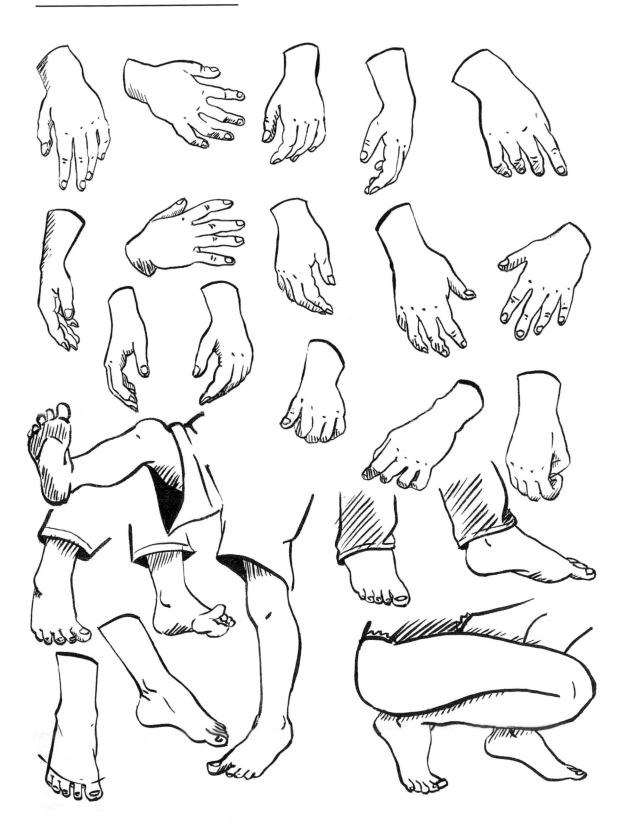

babies' hands and feet

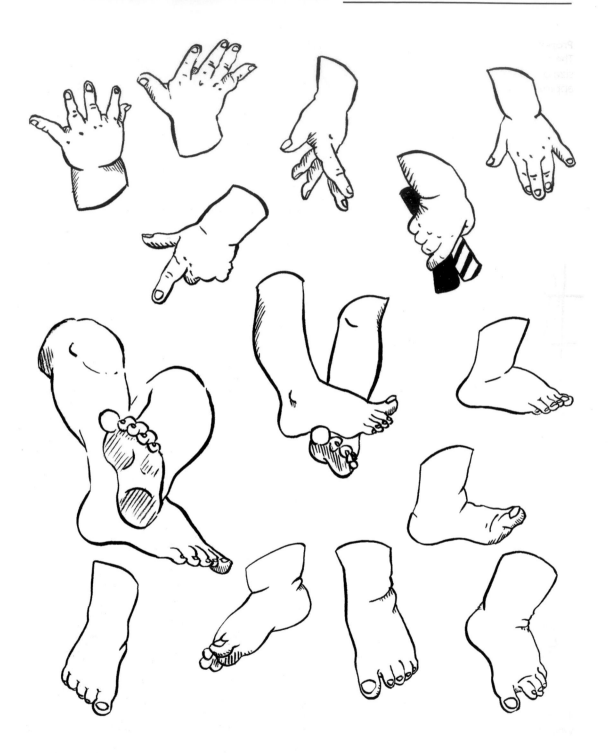

Proportion

The sole of the foot, not including toes is equal to the size of the head in adults (not children!). The big toe is approximately one quarter of the whole foot.

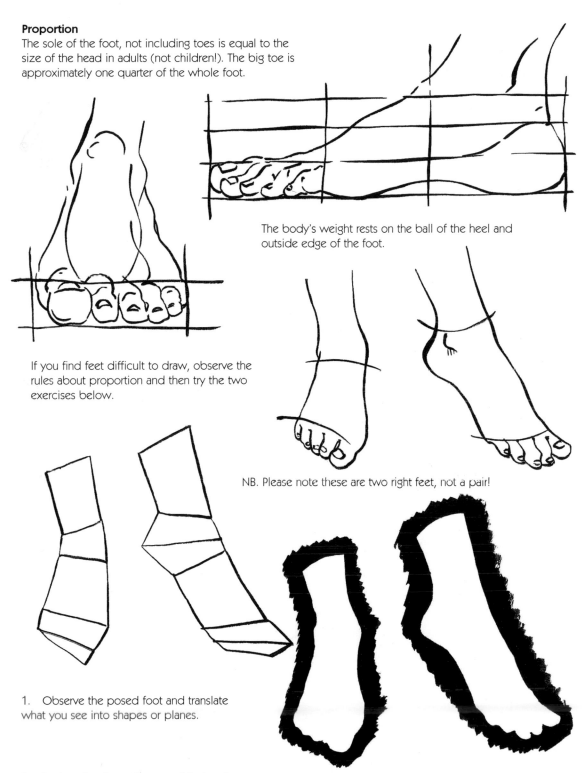

The body's weight rests on the ball of the heel and outside edge of the foot.

If you find feet difficult to draw, observe the rules about proportion and then try the two exercises below.

NB. Please note these are two right feet, not a pair!

1.   Observe the posed foot and translate what you see into shapes or planes.

2.   Look at the shape the posed foot makes in space and draw the silhouette only.

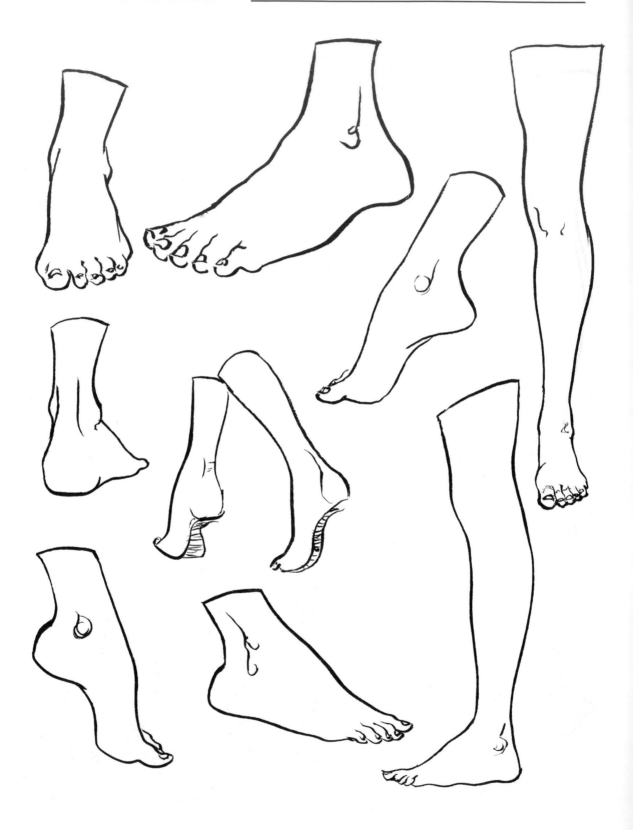

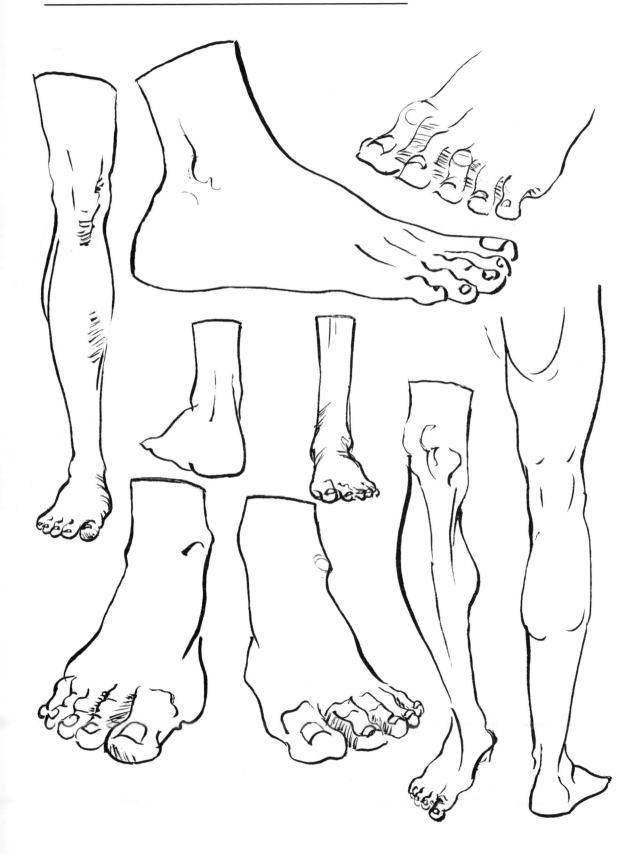

men's boots and shoes

MEDIA TECHNIQUES

The choice of technique in an illustration depends upon the final use of the illustration. If it is to promote an idea as an advertisement then a feeling for fashionable imagery and graphics is necessary. If fashionable imagery is slick and precise at the time, then your illustration should emulate that feeling or mood as well as promote the original idea. In contrast, if there is a feeling towards a natural, hand-made look, then again your illustrations should encapsulate that feeling. This is because there are 'fashions' in fashion illustration as well as any other changing product.

It is important to be observant of the world around you to understand any new feelings or changes that might occur and keep your drawings 'up to date'.

The illustration may be to promote your own personal style and help develop your own design ideas for a portfolio. This follows much the same line as previously, but also needs clarity for informing other people about your work. Consequently fabric representation may play a very important part, in which case it is important to choose the right technique. See next section on *Fabric Representation*.

Working/flat/technical/specification drawings need to be rendered with great clarity to inform adequately, as these drawings are seen by pattern cutters, designers, buyers, merchandisers, and other personnel within the industry. See section on *Drawing for Manufacture*.

The drawing may be for publication, where not only does it have to look fresh and exciting but it must also be prepared for reproduction, which may rule out certain techniques. It is best to discuss this with the publisher. Usually if the work photocopies well then it would be fine for printing.

The following chapter includes a variety of methods of rendering and presenting work. They are laid out in an accessible format and techniques can be combined as you wish. Each technique is accompanied by a recipe for the medium used, from basic pencil work through colour photocopiers to computer generated images. Along the bottom of each page is a visual checklist on the media being used on that page. The figure at the beginning of the chapter is to give the feeling of the full line drawing which is then experimented upon.

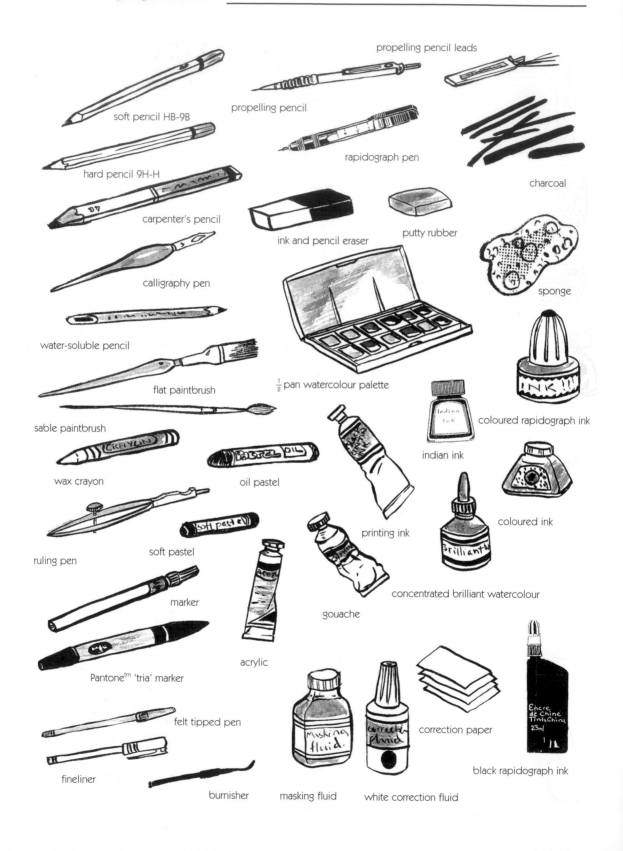

propelling pencil leads

soft pencil HB-9B

propelling pencil

hard pencil 9H-H

rapidograph pen

carpenter's pencil

charcoal

ink and pencil eraser

putty rubber

calligraphy pen

sponge

water-soluble pencil

flat paintbrush

½ pan watercolour palette

INK

coloured rapidograph ink

sable paintbrush

indian ink

wax crayon

oil pastel

printing ink

coloured ink

ruling pen

soft pastel

concentrated brilliant watercolour

marker

gouache

acrylic

Pantone^{tm} 'tria' marker

felt tipped pen

correction paper

fineliner

black rapidograph ink

burnisher

masking fluid

white correction fluid

printing roller

color tag™

colour printer

knife

computer

spray

self heal cutting mat

black and white/colour photocopier

light box

watercolour papers

cartridge, marker
and copier papers

fixative

hand-make paper

spray mount

french curves

glue stick

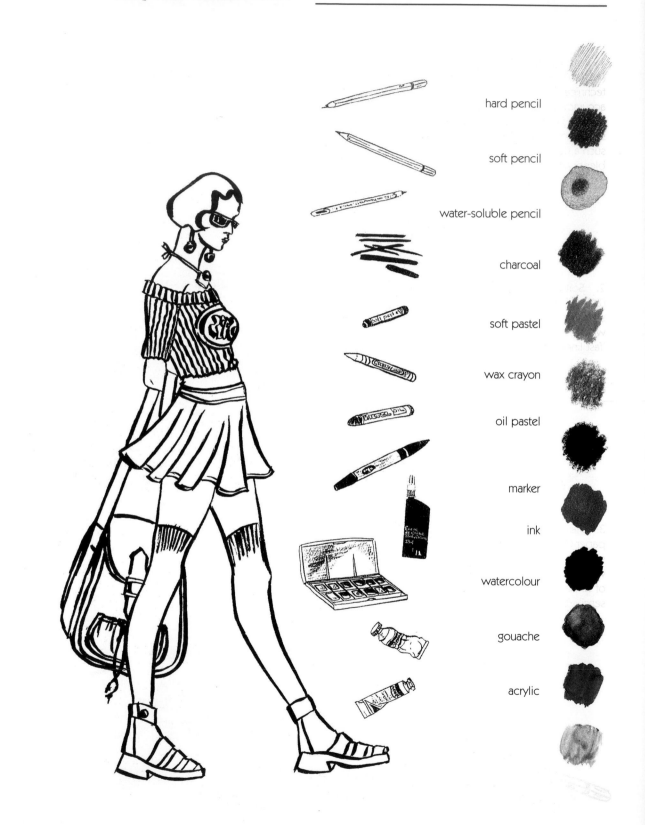

hard pencil

soft pencil

water-soluble pencil

charcoal

soft pastel

wax crayon

oil pastel

marker

ink

watercolour

gouache

acrylic

1.   Hard pencil (4H) on plain copier paper
(80 gsm). A hard pencil is generally used for
technical drawing and pattern cutting where
accuracy is essential. A smooth, flat drawing
surface, without texture, gives the most
satisfactory results. Plain copier paper is
such a paper, as is cartridge and
bleedproof marker paper.

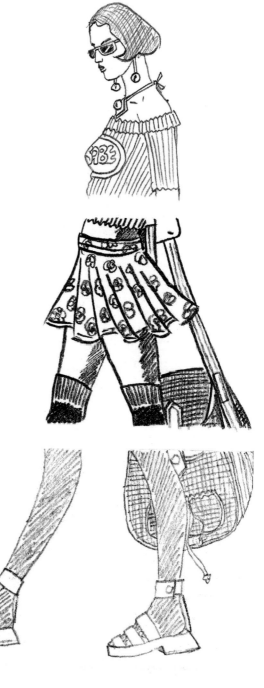

2.   Soft pencil (7B) on plain copier paper
(80 gsm). Soft pencils are better for
sketching, they give a very soft, black line
which is capable of showing sensitivity, i.e.
'fast lines' and 'slow lines'.

3.   Hard pencil (4H) on watercolour
paper (140 lb/300 gsm acid free, Not
surface). Hard pencil on a textured
watercolour paper tends to produce a line
of similar quality, there is not much
sensitivity shown.

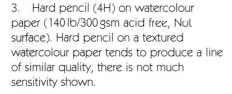

4.   Soft pencil (7B) on watercolour paper (140 lb/300 gsm acid free, Not surface). Soft pencil picks up the texture on a watercolour paper, giving a more varied line.

5.   Frottage using 4H and 7B pencils to take rubbings on plain copier paper (80 gsm). Frottage is an ideal technique to add texture quickly to illustration.

6.   Sfumato using 4B pencil for shaded background, 2H for outline of figure and hard eraser for lifting out shaded pencil on plain copier paper (80 gsm). True sfumato is achieved by allowing smoke to collect on the paper – this is a safer version!

7.   Very soft water-soluble graphite pencil, controlled with fine sable (size 2) brush and water on plain copier paper (80 gsm). This type of paper can handle small amounts of water before buckling.

8.   Very soft water-soluble graphite pencil, freely manipulated by random fine water mist (using plant sprayer) on plain copier paper (80 gsm).

9.   Very soft water-soluble graphite pencil, freely manipulated by random fine water mist (using plant sprayer) on watercolour paper (140 lb/300 gsm acid free, Not surface).

10.   Cross hatching using 4H and 2B pencils on plain copier paper (80 gsm). Cross hatching can be used in a variety of media, for example, pen and ink, coloured pencils, markers, rapidograph pens.

11.   Cross hatching using 4H pencil only on plain copier paper (80 gsm). Cross hatching adds texture, shadow and a three dimensional quality to illustrations.

12.   4B and 4H pencils using tone only, no line, on plain copier paper (80 gsm). This technique will work equally as well in full colour with coloured pencils, it gives a 'hazy' feeling to the illustration.

13.   Square tipped carpenter's pencil (4B) on plain copier paper (80 gsm). This pencil gives a blunt, 'square' line.

14.   Embossing/impressing using a fine, blunt instrument (here a propelling pencil without leads) on watercolour paper (140 lb/ 300 gsm acid free, Not surface). The paper needs to be quite thick to achieve success. 8H, 4H and 9B pencils were drawn lightly over the impressing.

15.   Three primary coloured pencils, red, yellow and blue applied to plain copier paper (80 gsm). The coloured pencils were layered to produce different colours (here viewed as tones in black and white!).

16.   Water-soluble coloured pencil applied to plain copier paper (80 gsm). The colour is then manipulated using water and a sable brush – do not over manipulate!

17.   Soft or chalk pastels on coloured paper. The pastels are at their most vivid and textural when applied to a coloured background as their opacity is obvious. The colour needs to be retained by using a fixative.

18.   Soft pastels are blended to achieve a three dimensional feeling. The best result is when three or four close shades of the same colour are laid down next to each other in grades from light to dark and are then blended together.

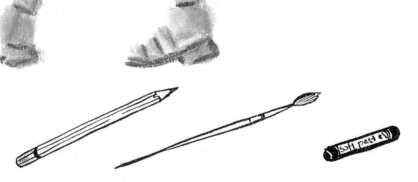

19.   Willow charcoal on plain copier paper (80 gsm) and fixed using a pastel and charcoal fixative. Charcoal is a good medium for sketching quickly and can be softened and smudged to achieve different effects.

20.   Oil pastel on plain copier paper (80 gsm). Oil pastel is very vibrant. It can be manipulated using a cottonwool bud and white spirit.

21.   Sgraffitto. White oil pastel laid down flat and black oil pastel laid over it on plain copier paper (80 gsm). The outline and detail is then scratched away, using a propelling pencil without the leads and a calligraphy pen nib. Coloured oil pastels can be used with spectacular results.

22.   Background is laid down as in No. 21. using white and black oil pastel. Plain copier paper (80 gsm) is laid over the top and a drawing made using a 4B pencil. The paper is peeled away and a print effect on the back of the drawing is achieved.

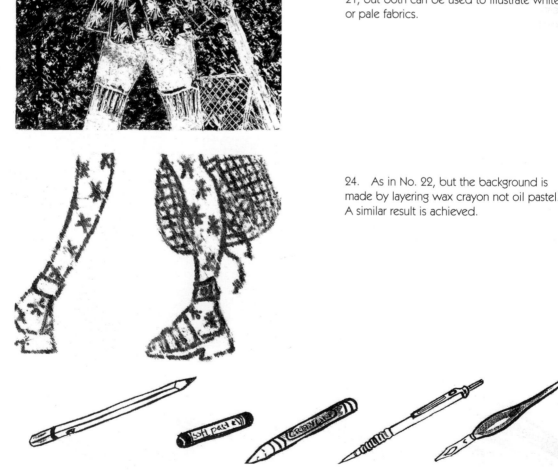

23.   As in No. 21, but this time using a layering of white and black wax crayon. The outline and detail is scratched away as before. The effect is more textural than No. 21, but both can be used to illustrate white or pale fabrics.

24.   As in No. 22, but the background is made by layering wax crayon not oil pastel. A similar result is achieved.

25. Markers laid down as flat colour on bleedproof marker paper (120 gsm). There are many markers available, the better art markers do tend to be expensive; cheaper versions are often difficult to lay down as flat colour.

26. Marker pens with colour blenders used as flat colour. The blender (usually found in children's stationery!) is laid over the top to create texture or pattern applied to bleedproof marker paper (120 gsm).

27. Marker pens laid down as flat colour on bleedproof marker paper (120 gsm) and worked into with pencil crayon to create shade, texture, pattern and/or highlight detail.

28.   Pantone 'tria' by Letraset® marker laid down as flat colour on plain copier paper (80 gsm). This technique is used frequently when illustrating active sportswear technical drawings. The 'tria' marker™ has three nibs – broad, medium and fine – for different types of work.

29.   Pantone 'tria' marker™ laid down as flat colour on plain copier paper (80 gsm). This paper does not bleed too much so it is easy to control the marker. The outline is rendered using the finest nib. Here shade is applied using a range of greys.

30.   The marker is applied flat on plain copier paper (80 gsm) but areas are left 'open' to create highlights. This technique could be combined with No. 29 to create a good three dimensional effect.

31.   Gouache laid down as flat colour on good quality cartridge paper (120 gsm). Gouache is an opaque paint made up of the same sort of pigment as watercolour, except that there is more opaque white added. It is ideal for developing colour stories and printed textile ideas.

32.   Gouache painted as line on good quality cartridge paper (120 gsm) using a size 2 sable paint brush. The paint colours available and gouache's good colour mixing qualities make it an indispensable tool.

33.   Gouache painted as flat colour on cartridge paper (120 gsm) and worked into with pencil and pencil crayon to create shade, texture or pattern. Gouache dries to a matt finish which allows other media to be applied over it.

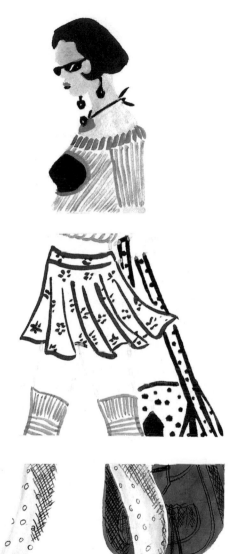

34.   Watercolour applied with a size 2 sable brush on watercolour paper (140 lb/ 300 gsm acid free, Not surface). The moisture is removed from the brush with a tissue or sheet of newspaper to achieve a textural brush stroke – known as the 'dry brush' technique.

35.   Wax crayon applied to watercolour paper (140 lb/300 gsm acid free, Not surface). Watercolour wash is applied to the paper, the wax crayon acts as a 'resist' to the wash. This technique can be built up in layers rather like a 'batik' effect.

36.   Masking fluid applied to watercolour paper (140 lb/300 gsm acid free, Not surface). Watercolour washes are added after the fluid has dried. When the watercolour is dry, the fluid is rubbed away. Layers can be built up to great effect as in No. 35.

37. Watercolour applied with a size 2 sable brush on watercolour paper (140 lb/ 300 gsm acid free, Not surface). The technique here is 'open line work' i.e. leaving space between each block of colour. Work can be speedily completed as there is no necessity to wait for each colour to dry.

38. A combination of 'wax resist', 'open line work' and 'wet on wet' – a technique where colour is added to another colour whilst both are still wet and the colours are allowed to run together. Watercolour paper is used (140 lb/300 gsm acid free, Not surface).

39. Wax resist and masking fluid applied as resists or masks on watercolour paper (140 lb/300 gsm acid free, Not surface). Watercolour is applied with a sponge and brush (size 2 sable) for texture and detail.

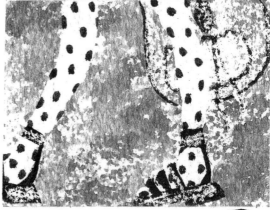

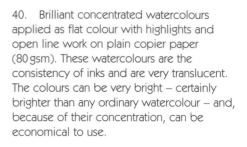

40.   Brilliant concentrated watercolours applied as flat colour with highlights and open line work on plain copier paper (80 gsm). These watercolours are the consistency of inks and are very translucent. The colours can be very bright – certainly brighter than any ordinary watercolour – and, because of their concentration, can be economical to use.

41.   Acrylic paint applied using a sable brush (size 2) on cartridge paper; stippling has been applied to the stockings. The texture of brush strokes can be very apparent with acrylics. They can be quite translucent or opaque.

42.   Acrylic paint applied using a sable brush (size 2) on cartridge paper. The bag was heavily painted and a sheet of paper laid on the paint and peeled away to remove some of the paint and produce a texture. The stockings were painted in a dark colour and then over painted in a lighter colour when dry. Before the second colour was dry it was combed with a hand-made cardboard comb to produce the stripes.

43.   Ink applied to plain copier paper (80 gsm) using a ruling pen. The ruling pen has a reservoir at the tip where ink is stored. The tip can be adjusted to achieve a variety of line widths. The pen is used as a dipping tool, consequently different coloured inks can be used as required. The pen needs the same sort of cleaning between colours as a brush.

44.   Ink applied with rapidograph/technical drawing pens (0.25, 0.35, and 0.50) to plain copier paper (80 gsm). Mainly used for technical/working drawings but also favoured in figurative work that is to be published as the ink line is opaque. They are more versatile these days as it is possible to use coloured and white inks in the reservoir as well as the standard black.

45.   Ink applied with calligraphy pen size $2\frac{1}{2}$ on plain copier paper (80 gsm). A calligraphy nib tends to be quite square to achieve the characteristic script writing. Here it is used to give a different line quality within the drawing.

46.   Ink applied with a size 2 sable brush on plain copier paper (80 gsm). The ink is quite opaque and photocopies very well. The ink is permanent and can be used with spirit-based markers, it will not bleed.

47.   Ink applied with a size 2 sable brush on watercolour paper (140 lb/300 gsm). The watercolour paper allows a certain amount of texture in the line. The ink is permanent and will allow watercolour paint to be applied liberally, the strength of the line should show through the watercolour.

48.   Ink applied with a ruling pen on watercolour paper (140 lb/300 gsm acid free, Not surface). The line becomes slightly scratchier due to the texture of the watercolour paper.

49. A stencil is made of the general silhouette; white ink is applied over the stencil onto a coloured paper background. Detail is painted in with a No. 2 sable brush. This is an ideal treatment for white or pale fabrics to show contrast.

50. White typing correction paper is used to draw on a coloured paper background; a very textural line is achieved. The shape and detail required is drawn on white paper and laid on top of the correction paper, which is laid face down onto the presentation surface, and then the outline is traced using a hard pencil.

51. White typing correction paper is applied roughly to a coloured paper background to create a texture and allow the sub paper to show through slightly, the result is then drawn upon with an HB pencil. The effect is like that of 'silver point' where a metal tip is drawn on a gouache base.

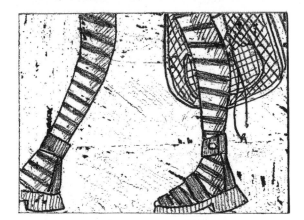

52.   Contrasting coloured paper (here a sort of sugar paper) is used to collage the shapes of the figure on plain copier paper (80 gsm) using a solvent free glue. A preliminary drawing is made that can be dissected to achieve the collage shapes. Space can be left between collaged shapes, rather like 'open line work', to achieve an effect of outline.

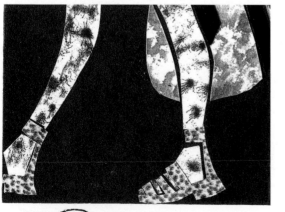

53.   The remains of the typing correction paper from No. 50 are applied to a coloured paper background; more detail is scratched away using a sharp knife.

54.   Textures and patterns are sponged, stippled and blown with ink and a straw onto plain copier paper (80 gsm) and then collaged for contrast onto a coloured paper background using a solvent free glue.

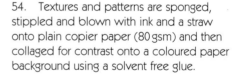

55.   Hand-made papers are collaged together and applied to plain copier paper (80 gsm) using a solvent free glue. As in No. 52 a preliminary drawing needs to be made that can be dissected to provide the shapes required. If the paper can be seen through using a light box, the task can be made much easier and quicker by simply tracing the shapes and then cutting them out with a scalpel and cutting mat.

56.   Newsprint is used as a collage medium and applied to plain copier paper (80 gsm) using a solvent free glue. The newsprint is randomly torn to achieve the collage shapes required. Different coloured backgrounds and type faces add variety to the illustration.

57.   Hand-made papers are collaged together onto a hand-made paper background using a solvent free glue, acrylic paint is then applied with a size 2 sable brush for outlining and further contrast.

58.   Coloured tissue paper roughly torn and collaged together, applied to plain copier paper (80 gsm) using a solvent free glue. The scale of the drawing does not allow a great deal of detail with this technique, consequently choices have to be made about the key details needed for a successful illustration.

59.   Coloured tissue paper cut to shape, collaged together and applied to plain copier paper (80 gsm) using a solvent free glue. Detail is painted in with bleach and a No. 2 bristle brush – do not use a good quality brush as the bleach will ultimately destroy it. Some coloured tissue papers show slightly different colours when bleached.

60.   The outline of the figure is painted with a No. 2 sable brush and black ink on plain copier paper (80 gsm). The stockings are filled in with black ink. The drawing is photocopied. Areas are then masked off using masking tape. Color tag^{tm} strips by Letraset® are applied where required using the color tag^{tm} machine. The principle is that wherever there is solid black photocopy toner then color tag^{tm} strips can be applied using the heat from the machine.

61.   The figure is painted with black ink on plain copier paper (80 gsm) using a size 2 sable brush. Letratone^{tm} by Letraset® is applied loosely and is burnished onto the surface of the drawing giving contrast and texture.

62.   The figure is drawn using black ink and rapidograph/technical drawing pens (0.25, 0.35 and 0.50). A variety of letratone^{tm} is then used in a more controlled way to the edges of the drawing. The drawing is quite flat but is clear and has contrast.

63.   The drawing is rendered with a sable brush (size 2) and ink on plain copier paper (80 gsm). Letratone^{tm} is then applied to give contrast and show highlights – the light source coming from the left.

64.   Plain copier paper (80 gsm) is randomly stamped using a stamping kit of ink pad and stamp shapes. If the illustration is not too small, your own stamps can be created using potatoes or sponges or lino. Once dry, the print is traced over to fit the illustration and is collaged into place. The drawing is finished using black ink and a sable brush to highlight detail.

65.   This 'monoprint' is produced by rolling water-soluble block printing ink onto a glass plate – a piece of perspex or glass from an old picture frame will work well. The plain copier paper (80 gsm) is then laid over the ink block and the illustration is traced on the back of the paper. When the paper is removed this is the result.

66.   This 'monoprint' is the same as No. 65, except that the ink block is blotted first to remove some of the moisture and consequently a finer line is produced. The water-soluble ink allows other media to be used on the print and also makes cleaning equipment much easier.

67.   A line drawing was produced using a sable brush (size 2) and ink. This was photocopied on acetate and gouache colour was applied to the back of the acetate wherever required. The acetate was overlaid on plain copier paper. Fine detail can be coloured using this method and it is ideal for printed textiles requiring black or coloured outlines.

68.   The same line drawing on acetate as in No. 67 was used here. Permanent markers of the type used for overhead projectors were applied to the acetate to achieve a transparent effect. Backgrounds could be effectively underlaid as a presentation technique. The colour choice in this range of pens tends to be limited.

69.   The same line drawing on acetate as in No. 67 was used here. Colour and texture is achieved by collaging fabrics roughly onto plain copier paper (80 gsm). The result, effective in its own right, is outlined on the acetate placed over the top. Larger illustrations are easier to handle!

70.   The same line drawing as in No. 67 is photocopied on a colour laser copier, but as a mirror image. The resulting image is swabbed with acetone (nail varnish remover) using a tissue or cottonwool ball, then turned face down onto a sheet of plain copier paper (80 gsm) and the back of the drawing rubbed down. The result is a fainter version of the original, but looks like a print.

71.   The same principle applies as to No. 70 but the substrate is a hand-made paper with a texture. The resulting print is more textural again than No. 70.

72.   The mirror image drawing of No. 67 is photocopied on a normal black toner photocopier. The image is then transferred using acetone (nail varnish remover) onto hand-made paper with a texture. The image produced is blacker in line but has broken up due to the textural paper. Pencil has been added to draw in the stripes of the stockings.

73. The brush and ink line drawing used in the last few techniques has been inverted on a colour laser copier, to produce a negative effect. This can be an interesting presentation technique, especially when producing a lot of working drawings.

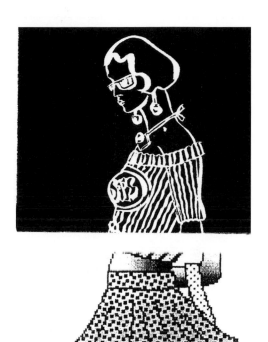

74. This is a computer generated image. The illustration was created, using the 'Claris Works, Paint' package, a mouse and an Apple Macintosh Performa. The package enables the illustrator to work with colour, gradients, patterns and textures.

75. A more sophisticated computer generated image. The line drawing in brush and ink from No. 67 and some fabric samples were scanned into a Power Macintosh. Through 'Adobe Photoshop' the fabric samples were reproduced onto the line drawing. Highlights were added to make the drawing appear more three dimensional.

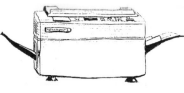

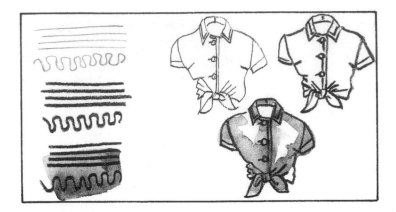

Pencil

The first pencil used is a 9H, a very hard pencil generally used for precise technical drawings. The second is a very soft 9B pencil used for sketching and ideal for producing a sensitive line. The third is an 8B water-soluble sketching pencil, giving a watercolour effect wash when brushed with water.

Ink

The first drawing is rendered with a 0.50 rapidograph technical pen, the second with a 0.25 rapidograph technical pen, the third uses a sable paint brush size 2 and the fourth uses a ruling pen. All are rendered in black rapidograph ink.

Watercolour

The first drawing is rendered with a size 2 sable brush and is 'open line work'. The second is a line drawing using the same brush but a 'dry brush' technique to achieve the tone (the brush is loaded with paint and the moisture is removed). The third is an open line drawing with a 'wet into wet' technique – colour is added whilst the original colour is still wet, just drop the colour in and allow it to disperse itself.

Markers

Here the Pantone 'tria'^{tm} by Letraset® is used to show the variety of nib sizes available. The first is the finest for detailed work, the second a medium sized nib, the third (the broadest) for applying a flat area of colour. The markers are compatible with photocopiers and laserprinters through the Pantone^{tm} colour system.

Letratone^{tm}

Sheets of self-adhesive tones and textures can be used in graphic work for professional presentation. Such tones are mostly computer generated now, but sheets are still available to buy in art shops. With these the image needed is cut from the sheet using a knife or scalpel, peeled away and applied to the artwork. It is then burnished into place to make it permanent and give a good finish.

How to apply letratone^{tm}

Using a light box and the design drawing, trace the shape of letratone^{tm} required either by using a pencil, or directly cutting the shape with a knife or scalpel. Peel away the shape from the backing paper and apply to the drawing where required. Finally, burnish the tone/texture permanently into place.

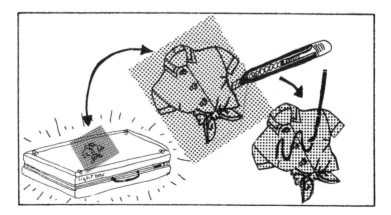

Computers
Tones and textures are found in some software packages and can be used to add pattern and tone to drawings. This example is from 'Claris Works'tm.

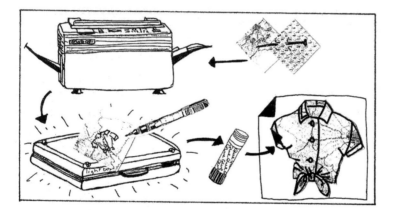

Collaging fabrics
The photocopier can produce copies of complicated fabrics which would be otherwise difficult to render. The fabric copy is traced over the drawing using a light box, similar to the letratonetm technique, but the image has to be glued in place, using a transparent glue or Spray Mounttm.

Reduction and enlargement
Photocopiers are an invaluable tool for an illustrator. Here scale is dealt with. The original is in the centre, the first is reduced to 61% and the last is enlarged to 141%. There are 1% increments between so that precise scales can be achieved.

Color Tag^{tm}

Drawings can be photocopied in black toner and colour can be added by means of the Color Tag^{tm} by Letraset®. Here colour strips (they can correspond to the Pantone^{tm} colour system) can be applied to the drawing using the ironing device, wherever there is deep black toner then the colour will adhere, changing a black line drawing to colour.

Papers

Finally papers – once the end use of an illustration is established ('before work begins!) then the substrate can be decided upon. There are many papers available for a variety of uses.

Here are examples of (clockwise) plain copier paper, bleedproof marker paper, tracing paper, acetate, two examples of hand-made papers, coloured paper – here sugar paper, watercolour paper, cartridge and in the centre a mottled calligraphy paper. Most suggest their final uses by their name, but it is possible to experiment with papers for different effects.

A summer wardrobe

Example executed using coloured and hand-made papers collaged with Letratone™. Background executed using Apple 'Quick Take 150' digital camera and printed, through an Apple Macintosh computer, in greyscale.

Example courtesy of Helen Pocock rendered in pencil and watercolour.

Example courtesy of Helen Farnell rendered in coloured pencil.

Example courtesy of Steven Tulip rendered in ink and watercolour.

Example courtesy of Milou Ket Styling and Design rendered in brush, ink and letratone™.

Marker pens used to free-hand sketch garments on the hanger.

Example courtesy of Nik Pandey, executed in soft pencil and frottage technique with acrylic paint, using a print technique.

Example executed on Apple Macintosh Performa with 'Claris Works' painting package.

Example executed on Apple Macintosh
Performa with 'Claris Works'
painting package.

FABRIC REPRESENTATION

One of the best ways to give illustrations 'life' is to research and practise representing fabrics. To illustrate the possibilities of fabric rendition, we have chosen to show examples of fabric representation in the restricted media of brush and ink, technical pen and soft pencil. See also *Media Techniques*.

Fabrics have texture, surface decoration and 'handling' quality. Rigid fabrics behave in a different manner to fluid ones. Printed fabrics looked at closely will take on a different aspect when seen from further away. (The scale of fabrics represented on paper is obviously different to the swatch of actual fabric.)

A good exercise is to paint and draw fabric samples to experiment with techniques for representing different effects and textures. The best practice is drawing from life, using a model, study the way clothes drape and hang on a moving figure, Working from magazines and photographs is a good second best.

Open your wardrobe and draw a selection of garments on their hangers!

Visiting any gallery will give an enhanced awareness of the skills artists have shown in representing fabrics, particularly cotton lawns, velvets, brocades and satins. This is a rich source for endless research.

The following pages illustrate examples of fabrics on the figure and as sample studies. There are examples of patterned fabrics, prints and embroideries. Complicated designs are simplified as necessitated by the confines of scale.

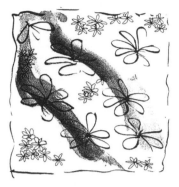

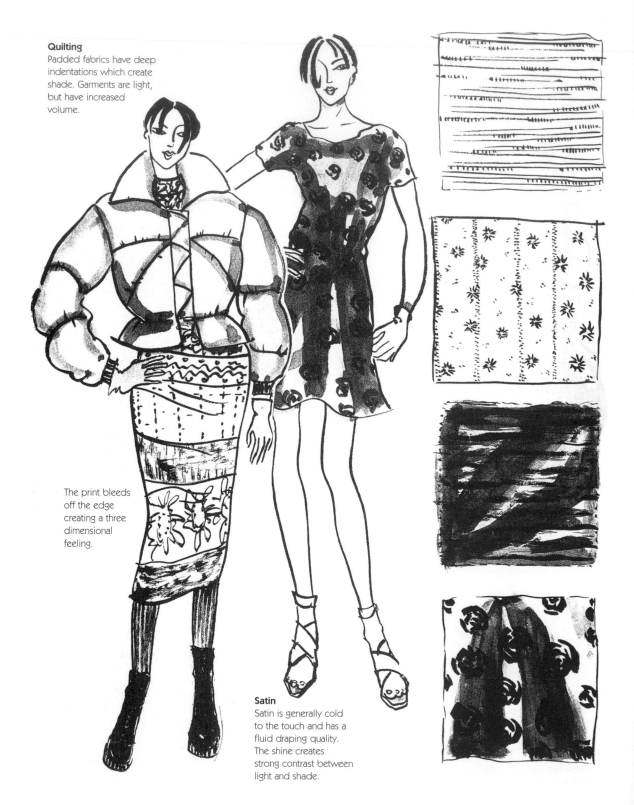

Quilting
Padded fabrics have deep indentations which create shade. Garments are light, but have increased volume.

The print bleeds off the edge creating a three dimensional feeling.

Satin
Satin is generally cold to the touch and has a fluid draping quality. The shine creates strong contrast between light and shade.

Faux fur
Deep pile fake furs have volume
and texture. The outline is textured
and highlights left to suggest gloss.

Organza
Semi-transparent fabrics
have a cloudy effect
drawn here with a dry brush.
Organza and taffeta are
stiff and light creating volume.

Prints
Folds can affect
the way a print behaves;
parts of motifs can
be hidden.

A soft pencil was used to draw a textured knit. Different pressure and a rough cross hatching suggest a woven tweed.

Mohair is open textured and voluminous. This effect was created by the repetition of a rubber stamp.

The texture of chunky knits needs to be contrasted, using light and shade in a broken, textured outline.

Textures can be created easily by frottage or stippling. See *Media Techniques*.

A cross lighting effect is used to highlight the texture of a patterned knit.

Boucle
It is sometimes useful to exaggerate texture like the tiny loops of boucle in order to create an effect.

Broderie Anglaise
Very simple marks on paper can be used to suggest certain fabrics.

Silk habotai
Drawn with line and wash.

Fluid fabrics which drape need to be drawn in a fluid manner. Stippling can indicate texture.

Rough textured knit drawn in 8B pencil using frottage.

Textured knit drawn in black ink and correction fluid applied with dry brush. Areas of white left to suggest the transparency of chiffon.

Examples of frottage and simple marks to suggest embroideries, textured weaves, terry towelling, sheepskin, etc. The dogtooth check is a photocopy of the actual fabric.

Faux fur
Heavy flicks of ink and areas of
white indicate rough texture.
Ink wash was used for shine
on satinised lycra.

Wool
Soft texture of woollen coat
drawn in 8B pencil.

Honiton lace
Brush and ink squiggles.

Smudged 8B pencil was used to emphasise the undefined outlines of a woollen coat. Pencil was applied over ink to suggest fake fur trim.

Examples of various treatments of one fabric type. Brush and ink, with stippling.

Transparency
Layers of transparent fabric like chiffon can be suggested by indicating separate layers at the hem, sleeves, etc.

Fluidity
Fluid fabrics will hang in folds close to the body.

Pattern and folds
Bold patterns, for example checks and stripes, show distortions in movement, creases and folds.

Fringing
Flicks of the brush suggest fringing; it has more life if drawn as in movement.

Velvets and velours
Napped fabrics like velvets have a
deep matt colour with no highlight
and a soft undefined outline.
Construction lines are rarely evident.

Jersey
Stripes distorted by movement –
folds suggest a simple jersey.
Not all fabrics have obvious
characteristics and some rely on
pattern or print.

Unusual 'fabrics'
Fabric constructed with metal discs.
Patent boots – white left for highlights.

Simple squiggles suggest 'mock croc'.

A simple technique for adding highlight is to apply correction fluid over a contrast ground.

Irregular pleating, like crystal, is drawn here with a dry hogs hair brush.

This representation is as
much about what is left
out than what is drawn.

Lace can be anything from
diaphanous to stretch, from
simple tulle to encrusted
embroidery.

A fine technical pen can be used
to draw delicate lace and a
brush to draw more robust types.

tulle

SKETCH BOOKS

Ideas and concepts

Sketching from life is an important part of understanding the human form. Keeping a sketch book is a means of practising the skills necessary in order to improve drawing and develop fashion awareness.

Visual notes can help to form design solutions. Designers take notes and sketches whilst on trips, from television, films, whilst shopping or researching, from books, galleries, etc. Sketch books can form a treasury of ideas to plunder – a visual diary of places, events, ideas, patterns, textures, form and colour. Drawing is a springboard to both design and illustration.

Visual information can be recorded just like verbal information, but in graphic form. Analytical drawings or sketches are often required in order to communicate information; in a shop report, for example, where accuracy and speed are vital, drawing is the aid to memory.

Sketches can indicate underlying structure, possibilities, etc. – or anything the eye cannot see all at once.

Analytical drawing requires thought, not just artistic skill.

Unconnected vague ideas and thoughts can sometimes only be progressed through working them out on paper. Seeing a collection of sketches, doodles, notes and scribbles can prove to be a link to a fresh idea or perhaps the process of drawing allows thought to take place in new ways. To this end the use of a sketch book is fundamental; new associations and understandings emerge as getting visual information down on paper rationalises random thought.

Extracts from Paris sketch book. Observational sketches of people in the street, galleries, paintings, sculptures.

Building a visual diary generates new ideas for illustration.

Shop or show reports

Information has to be reported immediately from shows, exhibitions and shops. Photography is usually unacceptable, therefore detailed, quick sketches, made on the spot shortly after memorising the image, are used. The key to this type of work is observational skill and memory. Written notes and diagrams are included. Often these visual notes are developed into more finished illustrations later.

stripe red
£18.00

£14.50

£20.00
black outs

mock croc

£26.00

white plastic
£18.00

metallic £49.00

bug eye £99.99

silver + black
£9.00

flower power £35.00

cream + silver
£37.00

£45.00

metallic
squares

recycled plastic
£32.00

Extract from Paris fashion exhibition sketch book. Visual notes recorded on site from memory.

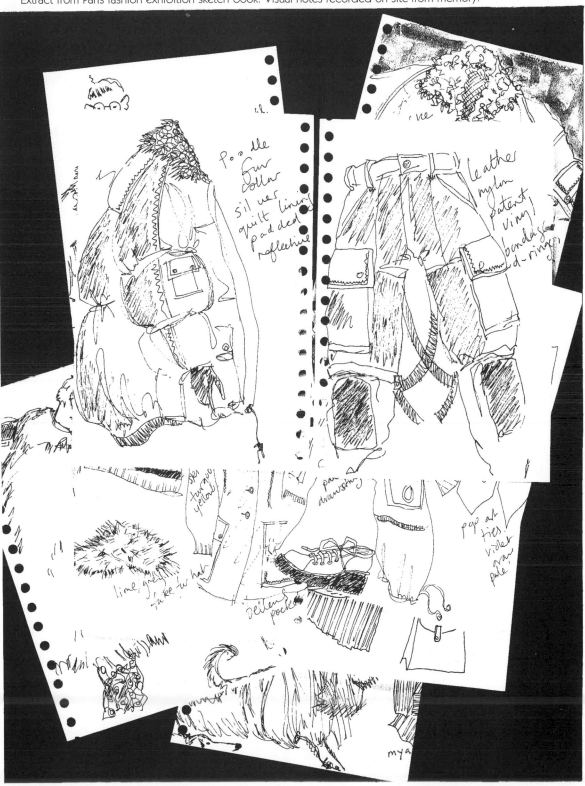

Extracts from designer's sketch book, drawings from memory.

Design development

Design development is the selection of sketch book research, to experiment and reach a design solution. Designers need to be able visually to communicate their ideas both quickly and accurately in order to progress their designs as they are drawn. One way to do this is to use templates of figures or garment types which can be roughly traced over, the design being changed and enhanced in the process. This method can be inhibiting, however, as it may limit the development of silhouettes and view points. Freehand design development becomes easier with practice.

Roughs.

cream/black
~~hair~~ hair press
3/4 coat.

Design development drawing using a basic tailored jacket shape to trace over.

Freehand design development drawings of similar designs.

This example was executed entirely on an Apple Macintosh Performa using 'Claris Works' painting package. This would be one of many design development sheets, using a variety of poses. One basic figure and one basic working drawing are repeated on this sheet with a different development each time, plus back views. This method of illustration is very efficient, but a good research sketch book is needed to help generate ideas. Refer to *Drawing from Life – Women's, Men's and Children's poses* and *Drawing for Manufacture* sections for advice.

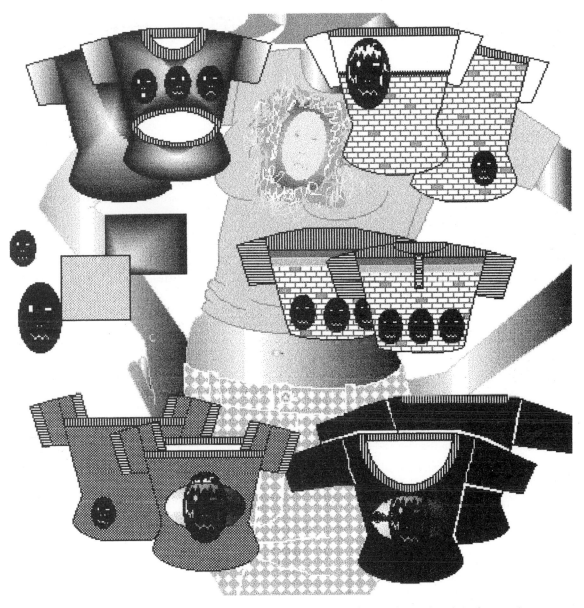

This woman's tee shirt design development sheet was executed on the Apple Macintosh Performa using 'Claris Works' painting package. There is a cropped torso illustration in the background to create the mood and working drawings (with front and back views) in the foreground.

FASHION ILLUSTRATION

During the first half of the 20th century fashion illustrations were widely used for features, covers and advertising in publications. However, the use of fashion illustration in commercial art has changed throughout the latter half of the 20th century from that of an illustration of an existing garment, to the communication and promotion of garments which are yet to be produced. The purpose of portraying existing styles has been largely superseded by photography. *Vogue*'s front cover was illustrated until 1936, when its first photographic cover was produced.

In the heyday of fashion illustration artists visited showrooms and studios of fashion houses where a mannequin would model the chosen garment. They then worked in their own time to produce drawings called 'croquis'. These were taken back to the studio and, using a light box, worked over and developed in line and wash. The illustrators' skills lay not only in drawing the style with artistic merit but in styling the drawing. The pose, model, hairstyle, etc. was skilfully rendered, portraying a typified vision of the look considered ideal at that time.

The great illustrators of the first half of the 20th century declined as patronage of their work ceased in favour of photography. Editorial work now forms only a small percentage of illustration. Fashion illustration for editorial will probably not revive as an art form under present circumstances. However there will always be a need for illustration to communicate design ideas, and drawing now more often fills the less prominent role of developing a design, communicating information for manufacturers, reporting and presenting trends and consumer information, promotion and advertising. Design and design issues are a part of the consumer society and commercial art has a value in itself as it reflects popular culture.

The essence of good fashion illustration is its ability to capture the spirit, the *zeitgeist* of the moment. To stay informed or ahead of contemporary trends is an art in its own right, demanding a certain amount of dedication The best sources of direct information are fashion columns in the broadsheet newspapers and magazines, and designer and specialist fashion stores in major cities. Indirectly there are general cultural sources – art, architecture, film, literature, street culture, music and sport.

Illustrations need not only be modelled by thin stylised women or men; surreal, unusual or witty alternatives can be more interesting and memorable.

Composition

Think about the abstract pattern that your figures will make on the page. Most pictures have a centre of interest – this often works better if not placed absolutely centrally.

Consider groups of models and how they will work together. There is no rule that groups have to be all on the same scale, or appear to occupy the same airspace.

Use contrast, light, shade and texture to add interest and drama. Try to think beyond lining up your models as if on a stage.

Fashion figures placed simply on the page.

The addition of various backgrounds completely alters the composition.

Repetitive imagery is good for consolidating a theme. Florals appear romantic.

Contemporary imagery can help to sell a mood.

Illustrations can be developed on a light box (or against a window) in order to change or stylise the drawing.

These poses, drawn from life, are developed and substantially exaggerated and demonstrate the process of stylisation.

The head size is reduced in a 10 plus head unit and the features are simplified and more heavily defined.

Illustrations abstracted from drawings from life.

Illustrations further stylised.

The same models can be dressed in an infinite variety of styles. When beginning to design, it is useful to develop a range of models and poses to enable a fast progression of ideas, rather than be hindered by difficult figure drawing problems. See *Drawing from Life – Women's, Men's and Children's poses.*

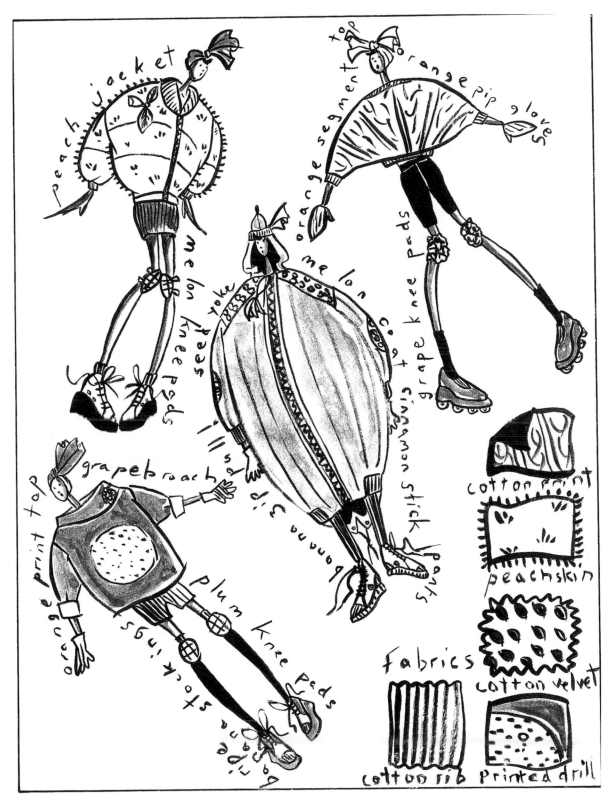

An example of highly stylised fashion figures used for quick realisation of a theme: a fun idea, but consider carefully who you present it to!

Drawing for promotion

Drawings are produced to promote or predict products for forthcoming trends. The prediction industry can only give an artist's impression of fashion seasons ahead; this is supplemented with photographs from the major international fashion shows. Illustration for prediction roughly falls into two categories:

- Drawings to illustrate themes, influences and directional looks. These tend to be the most contemporary of modern illustrative styles but with enough detail to convey the style adequately.
- Technical, highly detailed working drawings of garments, accessories and fabrics. Specification drawings (including measurements) are used by some companies.

A garment's life cycle begins with colour and raw materials which are processed, dyed and woven or knitted into textiles. In order to co-ordinate this huge industry consultancies provide information on trend and colour forecasting. Illustrations are used to promote themes and to visualise directional fashion trends. Consultancies also offer information, closer to the season, for designers and clothing manufacturers as a prediction or confirmation of these trends. Illustrations at this stage provide artist's impressions of garments which do not, as yet, exist.

Advertising and editorial

Although this role is largely taken over by photography, this is one of the few places where freedom of expression can be freely exercised. Graphic designers and more general illustrators are involved in competing for this kind of work.

Fashion illustrators are most often commissioned on a freelance basis by people qualified in fashion design, fashion marketing, graphics and fine art.

Here menswear is promoted through the sport of skiing: the theme name is 'Rescue'. Example courtesy of IN.D.EX.

Wind Block Cagoule

SILVER LINED HOOD

RESCUE Outerwear **10**

The working drawing is part of the 'Rescue' theme. Example courtesy of IN.D.EX.

A more sophisticated menswear theme is promoted here by accessories and pose. Example courtesy of IN.D.EX.

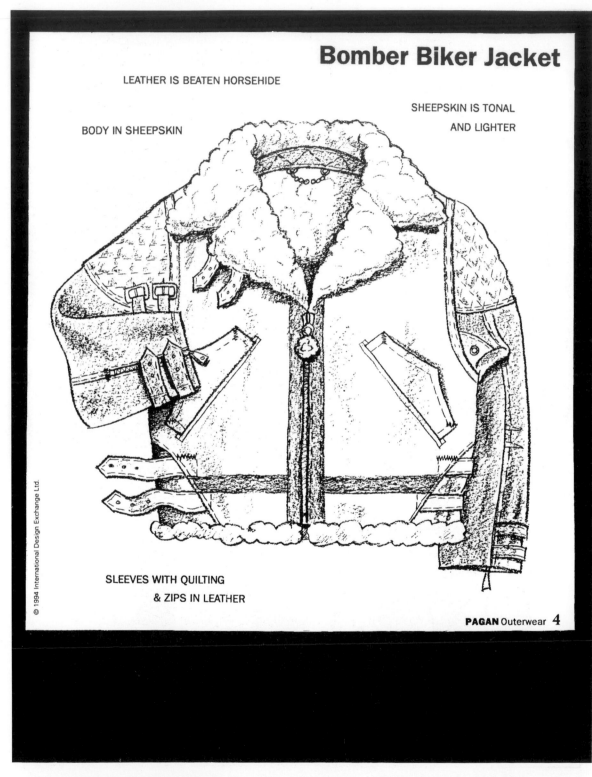

Bomber Biker Jacket

LEATHER IS BEATEN HORSEHIDE

SHEEPSKIN IS TONAL
AND LIGHTER

BODY IN SHEEPSKIN

© 1994 International Design Exchange Ltd.

SLEEVES WITH QUILTING
& ZIPS IN LEATHER

PAGAN Outerwear **4**

This garment is aimed at the winter season. Specific notations are provided regarding the fabrication.
Example courtesy of IN.D.EX.

CLASSICAL COATS

RHYTHM R & BLUES

MILITARY FORMS

4.22

Note the background to promote mood and the line drawing for detail. Example courtesy of Milou Ket Styling and Design.

Promoting men's loungewear with smiles and relaxed poses. Example courtesy of Chris Hogg.

Note the effect of simple composition and 'rugged' models. Example courtesy of IN.D.EX.

Note that the style of the drawing evokes the mood of the 1920s and 1930s. Example courtesy of Guerrilla Farm.

Note the natural proportions and pose of the bending figure and the unusual presentation of garment details. Example courtesy of Lisa Bratley.

Experimentation with the figure can help to promote ideas.

Drawing children

Illustrators and designers particularly stylise their drawings when drawing children, as it is often part of the marketing of that product.

Observing and drawing children from life and photographs helps towards understanding the different proportions of children at different ages and builds a knowledge of typical poses and actions.

Children will not sit still for long so you have to sketch quickly whilst they are at play, or catch a quieter moment sitting or asleep! Photographs are a useful reference but copies can look dull and lifeless when compared to the immediacy of a sketch from life.

Children's illustration/market

The childrenswear market is split into approximately three main age groups. From 0–2 years great development occurs: the baby learns to sit up, crawl and begin walking in approximately the first 12–14 months.

The next market level crosses over the first and runs from 2–8 years. At around the age of three the limbs become longer and co-ordination is improved. At approximately the age of four the child has a full set of 20 milk teeth and also starts nursery school.

The five to six-year-old begins to lose baby fat and the front teeth start to fall out! The rate of growth of the bones slows down around the age of seven and ten years. The adult teeth start to appear as molars. At seven years of age the brain begins to produce sex hormones and these increase in concentration over the next few years. This is a period when the activities of boys and girls alter and separate.

The last children's market ranges from 8–14 years. The rate of growth of bones starts to speed up again just before puberty. The child appears to be leggy and awkward. Different children start puberty at different ages, depending on the quality of their diet. At puberty the sex organs mature and secondary changes occur, that is, a girl will develop breasts and a boy's voice will break. See pages 50–63 for children's poses and proportions.

Observational drawings of children from life and photographs help with an understanding of proportion, poses and actions.

Brush and ink drawings developed from sketches.

A sketch book and worked up drawings from life.

1959

1928

1948

1966

Historical drawings and photographs can be used as a source of inspiration if a nostalgic look is required.

Stylisation of life drawings to cartoons.

Realism

to

caricature

Diagram to illustrate the process of stylisation, from realistic rendition to caricature. This process is applicable to all fashion illustration. The style and tone of an illustration depends upon the garment type, its intended market, contemporary trends and the illustrator's personal drawing style.

Examples of children drawn as cartoons.

Designers initial sketches of childrenswear collection – water soluble pencil.

Illustrations from a prediction publication,
courtesy of Milou Ket Styling and Design.

Designers freehand drawings, scanned into a computer program and flood filled with fabric and logo ideas. Example courtesy of Desmonds Childrenswear Division, executed on a PC (Personal Computer) using 'Windows' and 'Tex Design' software.

Illustrating garments and detail

The following pages provide examples of illustrations in a variety of different moods and seasons. As many situations as possible have been shown. Obviously the examples are not exhaustive but are a guide to illustrating garments that are reasonably fitted to the body.

The poses of a man, woman and child have been used to indicate how 'themes' in clothing are adaptable to both sexes and children when illustrating.

For simplicity and for comparison the basic templates here are the same but when starting out choose the right pose – does it convey the correct mood? If you are illustrating swimwear or lingerie, does the pose have good body shape and proportion? Hair styles and faces, and apparent age, are important also.

Shadows and tonal values can help to create a three dimensional feeling and clarify the design.

If a range or collection is being illustrated, then draw jackets and coats being held back by the model at one side to show the garments underneath.

Accessories can really consolidate a 'look'. Use them depending on the dictates of fashion.

A number of other tips are suggested with reference to the illustrations.

Stretch shorts and garments like them will be more convincing if the hem is drawn curved so that they appear to be wrapping around the leg.

Different line qualities can also be introduced by using technical pens – 0.50, 0.35 and 0.25 are adequate for conveying outlines, folds, details and topstitching. If budget is a problem fineliners are also available in different nib widths.

Draw garments so that they appear to be on top of the body, for example, if you are drawing straps allow the strap to be slightly proud of the shoulder.

Draw jackets and coats by observing how they really wrap around the neck and fasten, this is one of the hardest points to convey convincingly. If you can grasp the concept when pattern cutting it will become more obvious when illustrating.

Any garment with a wrap-over fasten, e.g. coats, jackets and skirts, will be more convincing if you draw the over wrap hanging slightly lower than the under wrap.

Use an imaginary light source to achieve more drama. Here the light is coming from the right.

To convey knitwear use ribbing, if it is part of the design. Different thicknesses of ribbing convey different weights of knitwear. Knitted garments without ribbing need to be drawn with a regular but textural outline, depending upon the stitch used.

If garment silhouettes are very simple and rely on colour to sell them, then use an interesting line for the silhouette, for example, ink and a sable brush produce very sensitive and variable line qualities.

Looser garments are more convincing if the back of the hem is visible, so that the garment looks like it is wrapped around the body.

Movement can be indicated by drawing folds in a full garment swinging in one direction, as if swept away by the wind.

Print and pattern can help to create a three dimensional feeling by being disjointed wherever a fold appears.

Depending on the fabric, weightier garments can be conveyed by using 'rounder' lines. The designs should also be illustrated as standing away from the body, as if layers are hidden underneath.

DRAWING FOR MANUFACTURE

This chapter deals with the 'working drawing'. This is the standard method of communicating garment designs in the industry. It is used in manufacturing to inform designers, pattern cutters, buyers, merchandisers, lay planners, machinists and any one else involved in the production of garments (some of whom may even be in a different country) about specific designs. Working drawings need to be clear to inform this vast range of personnel.

The drawings can be beautiful in their own right or perfunctory sketches done to explain the workings of a buttonhole in a busy design studio.

There is some skill involved in producing working drawings and this chapter sets out to provide the tools and knowledge necessary for successfully mastering the technique.

- **Basic equipment** gives an equipment list of items necessary to produce successful working drawings.
- **Drawings from the dress stand** are provided to be used as a basis for achieving good proportion giving guidelines for the centre front, back, bust, chest, waist and hips. Equally, a good, straightforward figure can be used in the same way. Men's, women's and children's body proportions have been provided.
- **Developing the template** shows how to achieve good proportion and how to develop a variety of garment 'blanks' that can be used as a basis to design virtually any garment. A range of templates for a five year old child, a woman and a man are provided as *Bodysuits and tops; Skirts, trousers and shorts; Full length coats and all-in-ones*.
- **Developing a stencil** provides another method which may be helpful if a light box is not available.
- **Designing using a template or stencil** shows how to illustrate design ideas using the blanks.
- **Rendering a working drawing** shows how rendering fabrics and details can make the drawing more interesting and relevant.
- **Explaining garment construction** helps pattern cutters and other personnel involved in the construction of garments to create new garment shapes by explanation through two dimensional drawings, this would be executed by the designer.
- **Where to use a working drawing** shows the subtleties between different uses of this type of drawing.

The examples at the end of this section show a variety of innovative and interesting approaches to this style of drawing.

Basic equipment

The basic equipment required for successful working drawings varies from hard or propelling pencils, rapidograph/technical drawing pens in a variety of nib thicknesses (or fineliner pens if budget is a problem), through erasers, ruling pens and a variety of inks. Black waterproof ink is useful as it is opaque when applied and reproduces well. Coloured inks are also available and can be used in technical pens. Correction fluid is invaluable to correct any slight inaccuracies. All-purpose fluids are available that can be used on photocopies as well as original art work.

Once the drawings have been rendered using the light box, then tones and textures can be applied using Letratone[tm], a sharp knife, burnisher and self-heal cutting mat. See *Media Techniques*.

French curves help to produce strict and accurate line work, depending on the final use of the illustration.

Technology is being used much more extensively in the fashion industry – Computer Aided Design. It is possible to execute working drawings and render them with tones, textures and colours. After the initial investment in the software, this is ultimately a more economical way of using tones and textures. It is also possible to scan in fabrics and flood fill them into working drawings to give a more realistic representation of the designs for presentation at buying and board meetings.

Drawings from the dress stand

There are a number of ways of producing good working drawings. There is a little preparation involved, but once this work has been achieved the results will last a very long time. If you are designing a range of garments and need to produce working drawings then it would make sense if each of the drawings was proportionate to the rest, that is, the garments look as if they fitted the same body. The following pages show how to achieve this.

The next three pages are drawings from the dress stand, including back, front and side views. The dress stand is ideal to use as a basis to develop working drawings as there is information regarding the centre front and back positions, the bust, waist and hips.

There are men's, women's and children's figures. Each has been presented as closely as possible in proportion to the next.

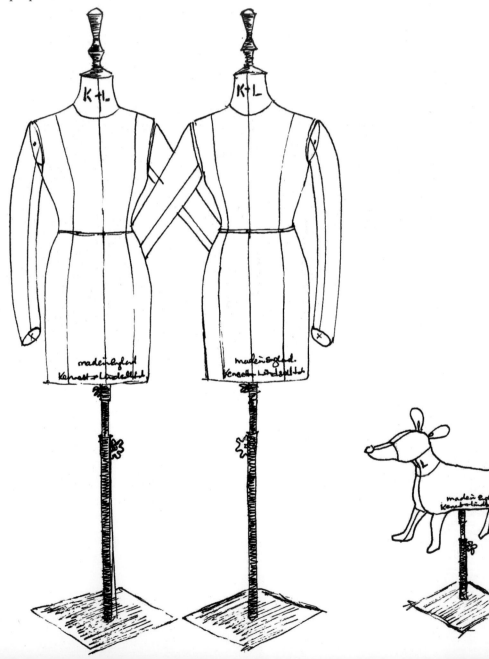

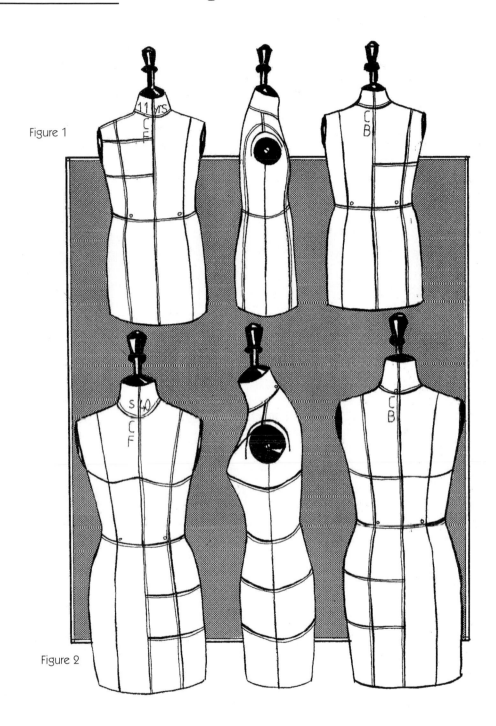

Figure 1

Figure 2

Figure 1 shows an 11 year old torso, Figure 2 a size 12 or 40 woman's torso.

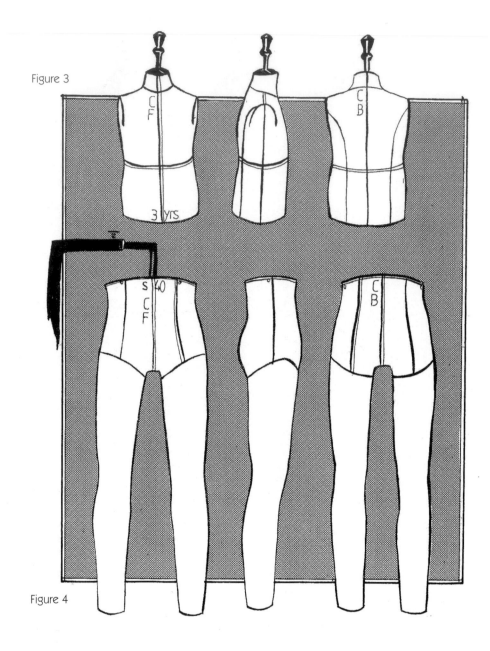

Figure 3

Figure 4

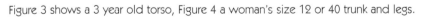

Figure 3 shows a 3 year old torso, Figure 4 a woman's size 12 or 40 trunk and legs.

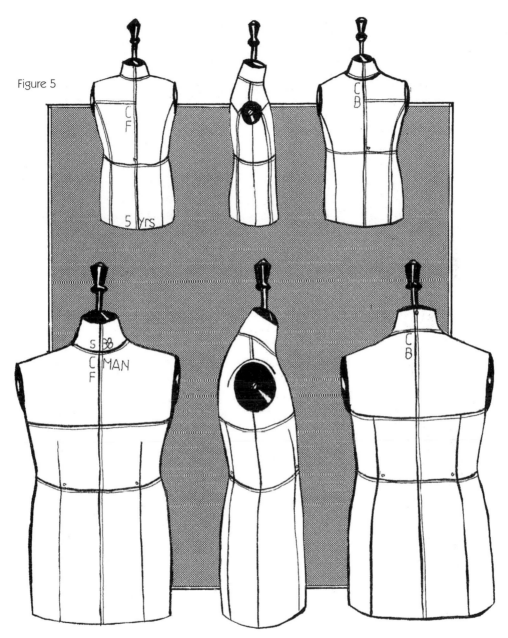

Figure 5

Figure 6

Figure 5 shows a 5 year old torso and Figure 6 a size 38 man's torso.

Developing the template

The woman, man and 5 year old child torso have been selected for development. Figure A is a combination of woman's torso and trunk and legs. This figure has been extended at the bust, waist, thigh and calf to allow for the elongation in fashion drawing. Figure B (man's torso) has been extended for the same reason, showing divisions at the chest, waist and hip. However, Figure C (child's torso – 5 years) has not been extended because this would alter the apparent age of the child and distort the proportions.

The trunk and legs have been returned back to the non-elongated proportion for the child's template and have been reduced in scale to fit the torso of the child at the waist. The man's legs have been developed from the woman's trunk and legs, again starting from the waist. The elongated proportions have been kept and some of the shaping has been altered slightly to look more masculine.

Front view templates are developed from the new figure shapes; back or side views can be developed using the same method described. A bodysuit is produced first, hugging the figure. Subsequent garments are presented as layers slightly larger than the last, as if they were garments worn on top of each other.

Sleeve shapes are developed. Tailored jackets have sleeves lying parallel to the body; with more casual sportswear, shirts and dresses allow the sleeves to spread at an angle from the body. (This is also dependent on the type of sleeve to be constructed. For example, a dolman sleeve is an extension of the body and the shoulder seam continues down the outside of the arm. Consequently the template chosen should be the nearest to that type of construction.) Where space on the page is at a premium one sleeve can be folded over; this allows detail at the back of the cuff to be seen.

Each template needs to retain information regarding the *centre front* and *back* and the *chest*, *bust*, *waist* and *hip lines* as this is helpful when plotting button wraps, double-breasted designs, wrap-overs, hipster styles, cropped tops, etc.

Once the templates have been produced (bodysuit, top, jacket, dress, skirt, trousers, coat and all-in-one) then a light box is needed to design garments on the templates.

Key

CF   Centre Front
BL   Bust Line
CL   Chest Line
WL   Waist Line
HL   Hip Line
Wrap   This is to aid in positioning the button wrap, which may be as wide as you wish depending on the size of the button.

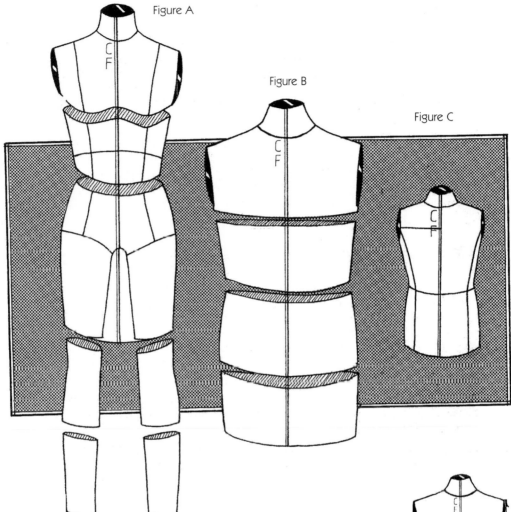

The 5 year old child's and man's torsos have legs added,
derived from the woman's.

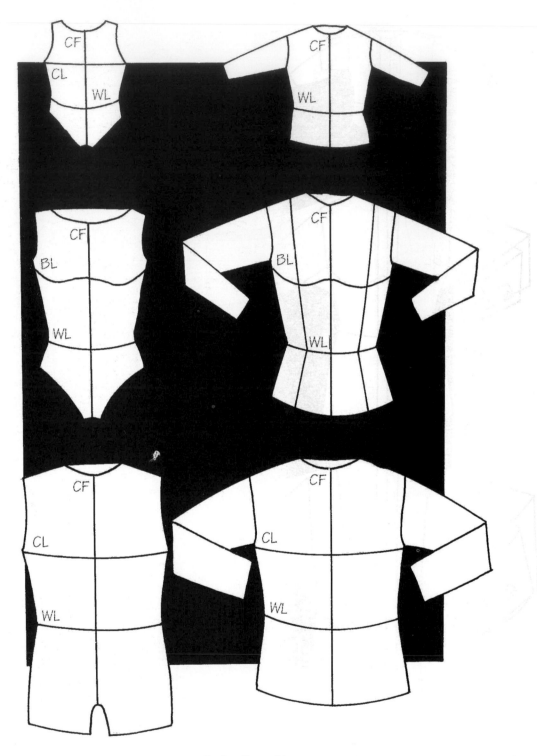

Bodysuits and tops

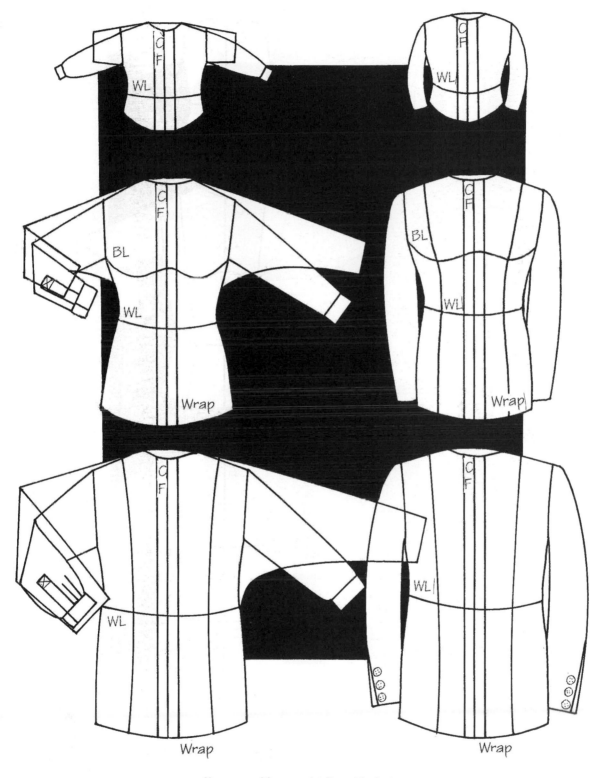

Sleeve positions and tailored jackets

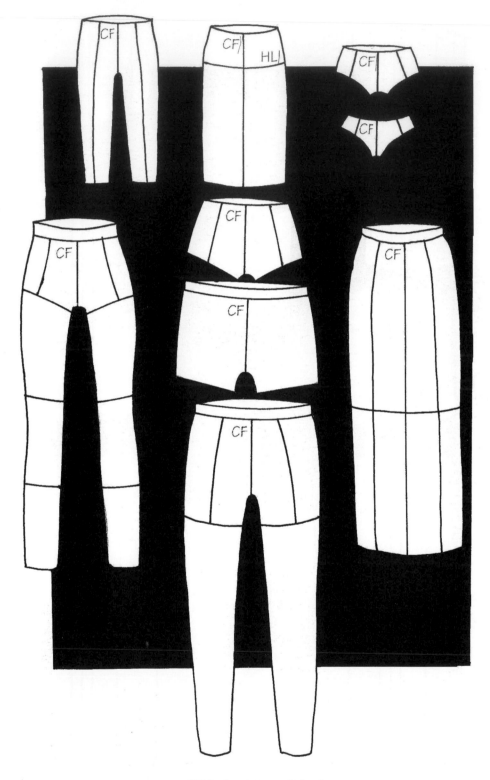

Skirts, trousers and shorts

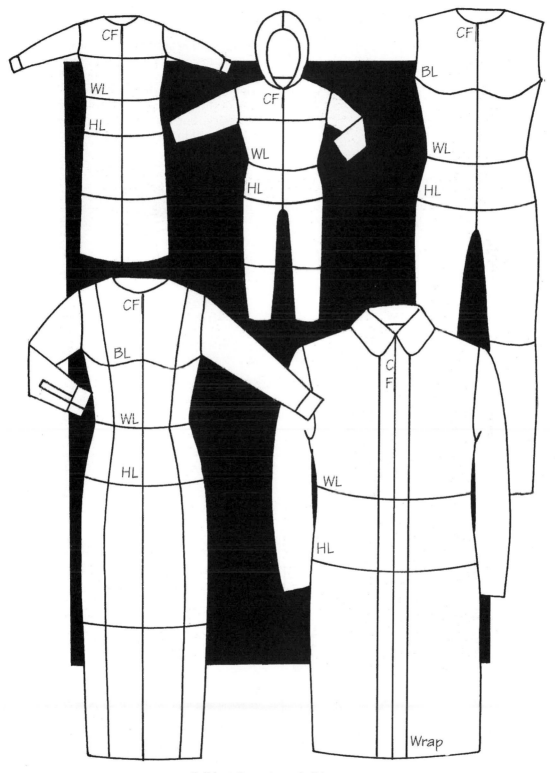

Full length coats and all-in-ones

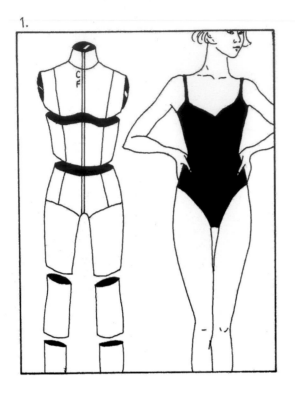

Developing a stencil

An alternative approach is that of producing stencils instead of templates, then drawing around the basic shape, lightly in pencil, which can then be designed upon. The advantage of this method is that a light box is not necessary, but it is important to use an 'H' value pencil to keep the traced shape as accurate as possible.

1.   Select the elongated dress stand drawing or a very clear front view of the figure.

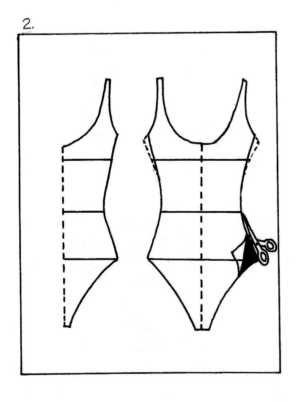

2.   Trace over one half of the torso to produce a swimsuit shape. Mirror the other side of the drawing and include the *centre front* or *back, chest* or *bust, waist* and *hip lines*. Adjust the shape slightly until it looks as required. Cut out the basic stencil, in lightweight card for durability. Further stencils can be created by working one on top of another to build up the layering effect.

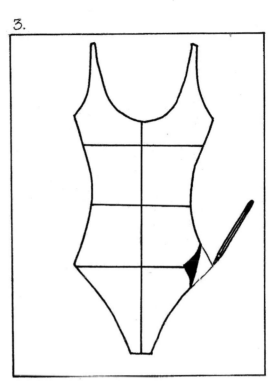

3.   To design, draw lightly around the basic stencil marking the centre front or back, chest or bust, waist and hip lines to use as guides.

4.   Design the garment over the tracing and render as required. Erase all pencil lines.

Design with a template or stencil

There follow examples of designing a woman's fitted jacket and a child's hooded anorak, using a template or stencil.

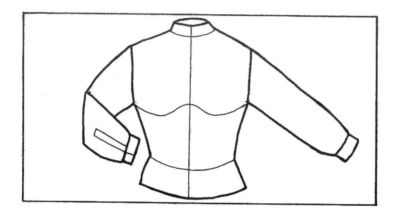

Select the relevant stencil or template required. This template is a fitted shirt which will be used to design a fitted jacket.

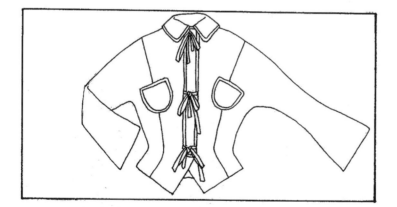

Draw the design silhouette and detail lightly over the stencil or template.

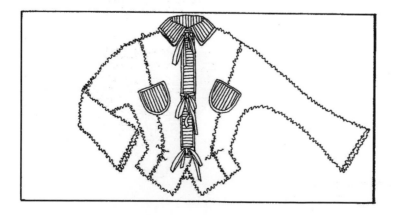

Render the fabrication by using line (here a towelling effect with knitted ribs). See *Fabric Representation*. Add colour if required.

1.
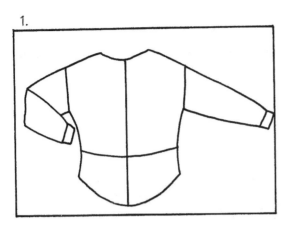

2.
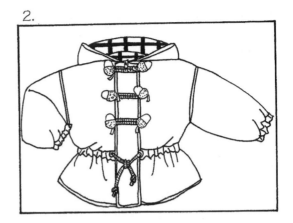

1. Select the relevant template/stencil and design.
2, 3, & 4.   Illustrate the front, back and side views to show the hood and garment silhouette.

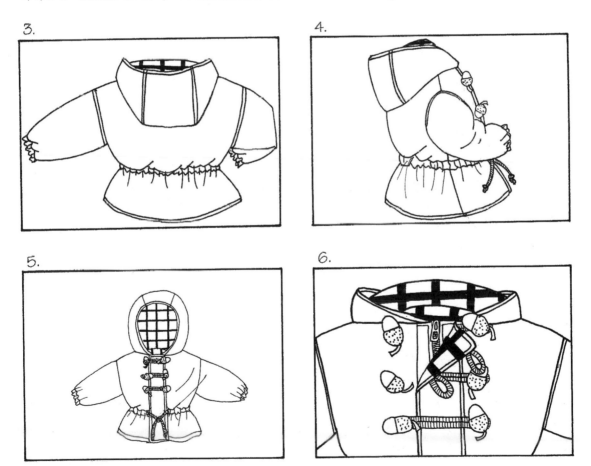

5.   Show the garment with the hood in wearing position, to illustrate the proportion.
6.   Draw a blown up detail of how the fastening works.

Rendering a working drawing

Rendering fabric convincingly is important in illustrating design ideas. Texture and pattern (see *Fabric Representation*) help to add interest to the drawing, whether it be for a figurative illustration or a working drawing for prediction use.

Plain **Transparent**

Knitted **Printed**

Looped **Fur**

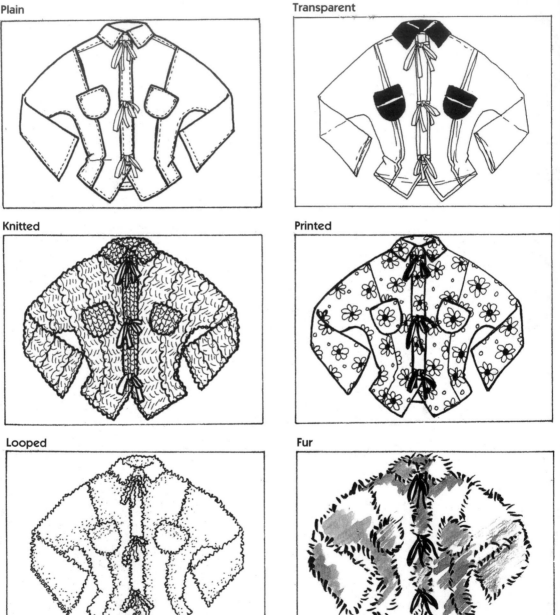

The **Plain** fabric is indicated by means of topstitching, the **Transparent** fabric by an ink wash, the **Knitted** by a textural silhouette and pattern, the **Printed** by allowing the pattern to bleed off the edge, the **Looped** effect by a textural silhouette and the **Fur** with brush, ink and wash.

Fun fur

Astrakhan fur

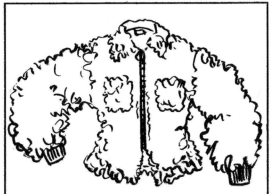

Padded

Quilted

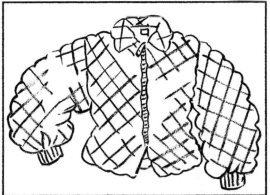

Fleece

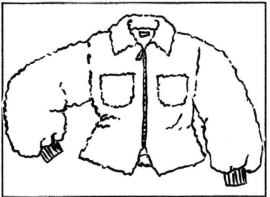

Knitted ribs

Fun fur rendered with a textural line, the garment looks bulky. For **Astrakhan fur** the textured line is looped like a sheep but is less bulky as the loops are close to the skin. The **Padded** garment is very rounded and bulky. The **Quilted** garment has stitch lines which can be in any design – this is traditional. The **Fleece** has a slightly textural line and the **Knitted rib** shows two contrasting ribs. All are executed with brush and ink.

Tweed

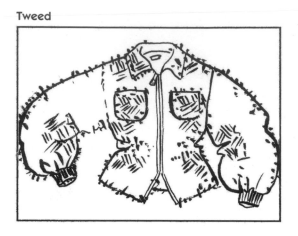

Fortuny style pleating

Organza

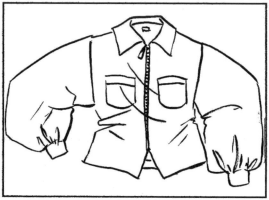

Velvet

Viscose

Stretch

The **Tweed** is rendered as a hairy line with textured patches. **Fortuny style pleating** gives a more delicate outline and less bulky silhouette. **Organza** gives a crisp silhouette. **Velvet** is rendered with a slightly dry brush and heavy line. **Viscose** is light and fluid and is rendered here with folds and a medium weight line. **Stretch** is rendered as a slimmer version of the garment with creasing at the waist. All are executed with brush and ink.

Technical drawings can be scanned into a computer and colours, pattern and text can be added in any configuration very quickly and efficiently. Fabrics or any image can be scanned directly into the programme and added to the drawing or design.

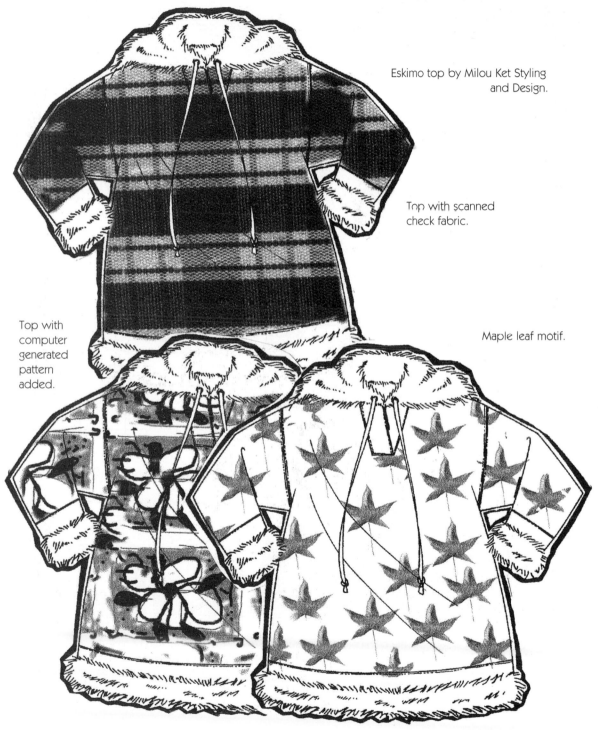

Eskimo top by Milou Ket Styling and Design.

Top with scanned check fabric.

Top with computer generated pattern added.

Maple leaf motif.

To explain construction

To illustrate hidden layers

This type of drawing is valuable in communicating information about the construction of a new garment silhouette, as here, using draping. It can be helpful in visualising further design ideas and thought processes.

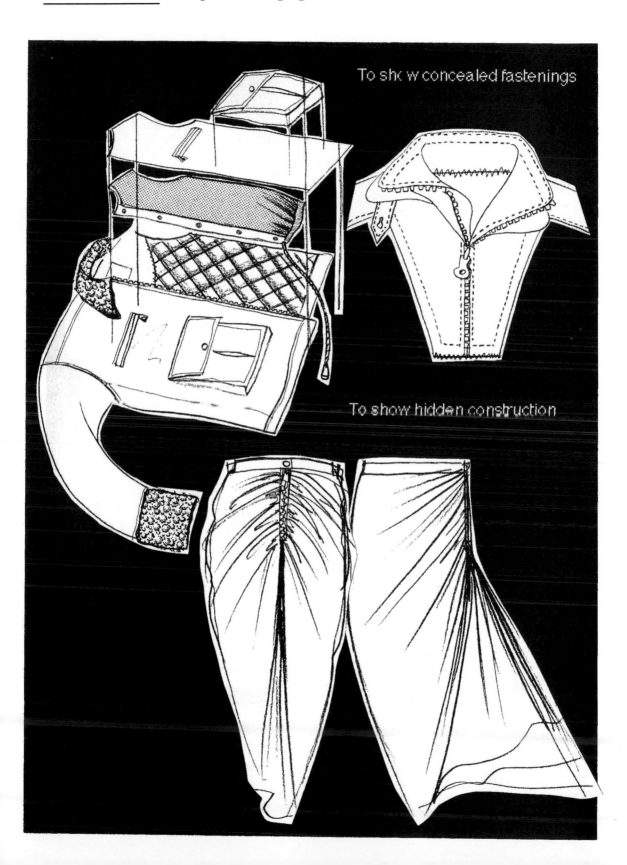

To show concealed fastenings

To show hidden construction

Where to use a working drawing

1.   The drawing is flat but has some movement indicated. The fabric representation is important. It is used here to illustrate items for fashion prediction work. Often important details will be highlighted in an exploded drawing.

SOURCE: _____

COUNTRY: _____

COLOUR: _____

FABRIC: _____

PRICE: _____

MARKET: _____

2.   A slightly stricter version of the working drawing used by fashion prediction and design studios. The garment has to be accurately observed and recorded. It could be derived from a trade fair or exhibition or could be from a retail outlet anywhere in the world. There has to be additional information such as the source or designer, country of manufacture, colour, fabric, price and market level. The prediction company uses such information to advise of directional garments corresponding to their previously predicted themes. The designer (depending on market level) may use the same directional information but is more likely to use the drawing technique to record comparitive information, that is, finding out what the competition is producing and comparing the product.

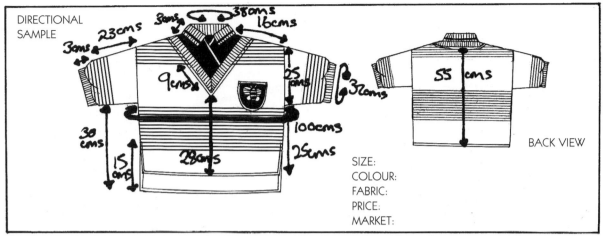

3. The drawing is the same in approach as No. 2, except that there is the addition of measurements. The garment would have been chosen for its directional qualities and would have been analysed and measured as a sample. Further information is required here regarding the size, colour, fabric, price and market level.

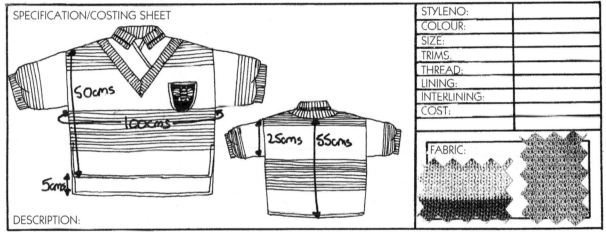

4. The drawing has to be clear with some key measurements to aid the pattern cutter on a specification sheet. It will also be used when costing out the produced garment.

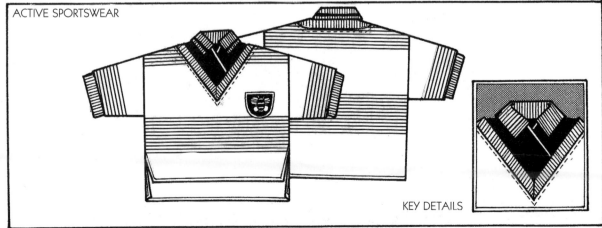

5. A more accurate version of the drawing is necessary when designing active sportswear; key details would also be included. French curves and templates may be used here and in Nos. 2, 3, and 4 to achieve clean and clear lines. See also *Specialist Areas*.

Example courtesy of Milou Ket Styling and Design.

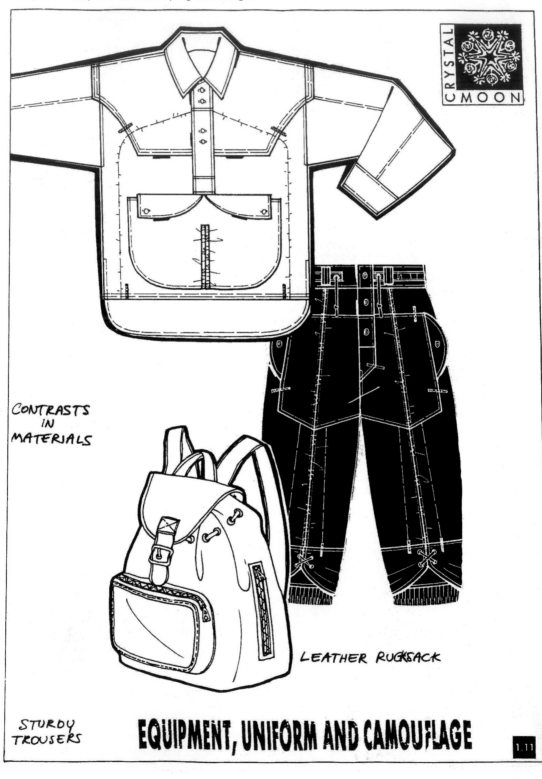

CRYSTAL
MOON

CONTRASTS
IN
MATERIALS

LEATHER RUCKSACK

STURDY
TROUSERS

EQUIPMENT, UNIFORM AND CAMOUFLAGE

1.11

Example courtesy of Janice Chadfield.

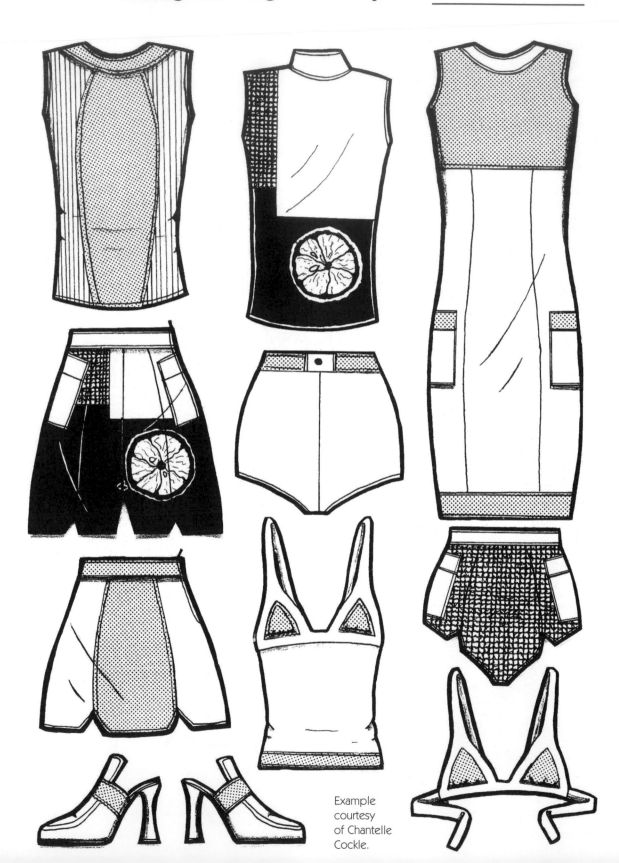

Example
courtesy
of Chantelle
Cockle.

Example executed on Apple Macintosh Performa with 'Claris Works' painting package.

Example courtesy of Helen Pocock.

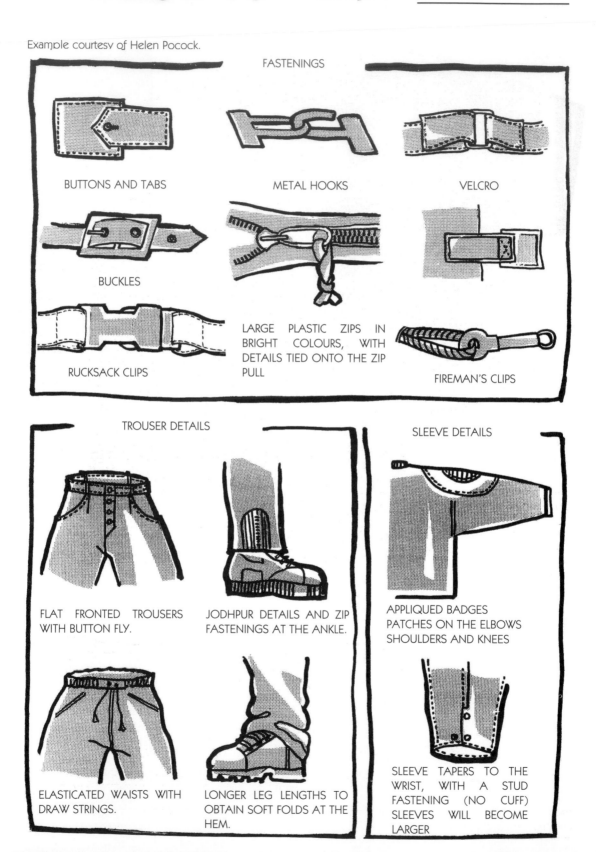

FASTENINGS

BUTTONS AND TABS

METAL HOOKS

VELCRO

BUCKLES

LARGE PLASTIC ZIPS IN BRIGHT COLOURS, WITH DETAILS TIED ONTO THE ZIP PULL

RUCKSACK CLIPS

FIREMAN'S CLIPS

TROUSER DETAILS

FLAT FRONTED TROUSERS WITH BUTTON FLY.

JODHPUR DETAILS AND ZIP FASTENINGS AT THE ANKLE.

ELASTICATED WAISTS WITH DRAW STRINGS.

LONGER LEG LENGTHS TO OBTAIN SOFT FOLDS AT THE HEM.

SLEEVE DETAILS

APPLIQUED BADGES PATCHES ON THE ELBOWS SHOULDERS AND KNEES

SLEEVE TAPERS TO THE WRIST, WITH A STUD FASTENING (NO CUFF) SLEEVES WILL BECOME LARGER

Example courtesy of Desmonds Childrenswear Division, executed on a PC with 'Windows' operating system and 'Tex Design' software.

Example courtesy of Desmonds Childrenswear Division, executed on a Silicon Graphics computer running 'CDi' and 'U4ia' software.

Example courtesy of IN.D.EX.

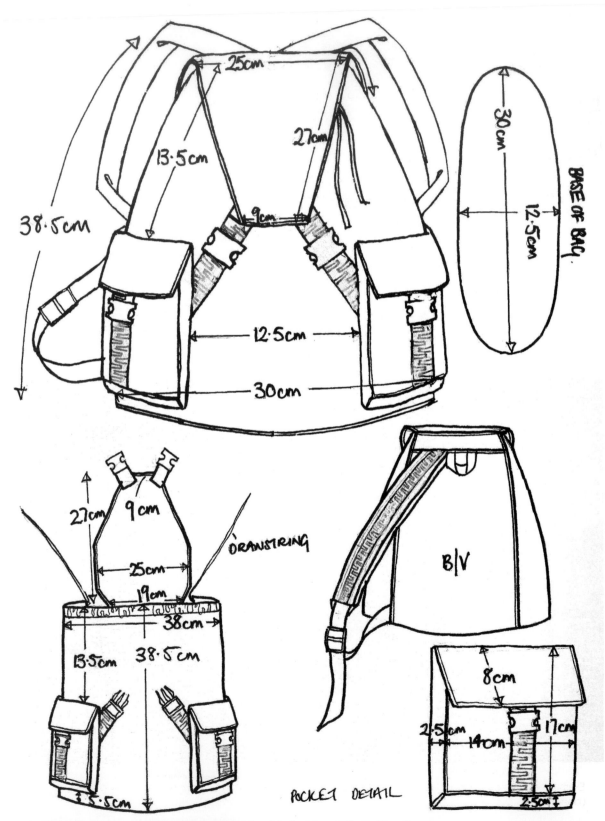

25cm

27cm

13.5cm

38.5cm

9cm

12.5cm

30cm

BASE OF BAG.

30cm

12.5cm

27cm

9cm

DRAWSTRING

25cm

19cm

38cm

38.5cm

13.5cm

5.5cm

B/V

8cm

2.5cm

17cm

14cm

2.5cm

POCKET DETAIL

Example courtesy of Sally Craig and Fiona Raeside for Newcastle Fashion Centre.

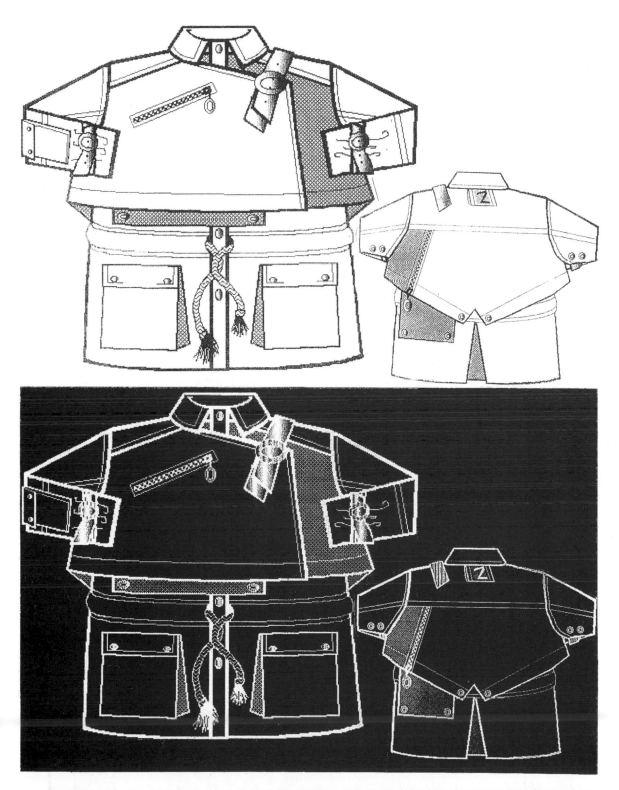

Example executed on Apple Macintosh Performa with 'Claris Works' painting package – drawing is inverted (bottom).

Example
courtesy
of Milou Ket
Styling
and Design.

SPECIALIST AREAS

When illustrating design or promotional ideas for a particular area, for example, maternity, active sportswear, lingerie/swimwear or accessories, it is important to research the area as thoroughly as time will allow. This would entail visiting shops and stores stocking items in the specialist area and observing how they are selling them. Is it through photographic styling? Is it through point of sale leaflets? Is it through catalogues? Photography will probably be the key selling medium. Look at the styling of the photography, look at the type of models being used and the kind of activities they are engaged in, and look at the way the shop displays merchandise.

Get a 'feeling' for contemporary promotional techniques in the specialist area. Use a small notebook to record key information (see section on *Sketch Books*), whether it is as an actual shop report to help in designing, or promotional information to help in the illustrating of the design.

Collect contemporary visuals of models at the correct market level for the specialist area. Specialist magazines are perfect for maternity wear and active sportswear; fashion magazines and catalogues are ideal for lingerie/swimwear and accessories. Practise drawing using the visuals and develop poses/figures for designing.

Some of the specialist areas have specific activities (active sportswear, cycling, football, snakeboarding, skating, etc.) which can be stylised and presented to consolidate the illustration. Be careful not to overdo this, though, the danger being that the design may be overshadowed.

Maternity

The approach to illustrating for maternity wear should revolve around the shape and stance of the figure – for obvious reasons! The needs of a woman in the late stages of pregnancy should have been discovered at the design stage. This is helpful information for illustration purposes also. Fashion input is important and illustrations should reflect this. A pregnant woman is as fashion-conscious as she was before her pregnancy and so any promotional illustration should consider this. See *Maternity* in this section for a variety of poses.

Active sportswear

Illustrating active sportswear requires attention to detail. Silhouettes of garments do not change very quickly. The design content may be a self-coloured jacquard woven or knitted into fabric, or possibly the placement and scale of logos. Sponsors of particular sports require their name to be visible somewhere within designs and there are limitations also, for example, with football shirts. There are many other considerations, most requiring great attention to detail when illustrating new ideas. See *Active sportswear* in this section. Sports shoes are evolving and shapes are becoming quite radical, depending upon the sport. There can be a great deal of detail evident in these shoes and this has to be shown at the design level.

Detailed illustrations also have to be rendered in colour. This tends to be applied very flat so that the detail is not obscured. Broad tipped marker pens tend to be the easiest solution to the problem, but using them is also a skill, see *Colour blocking* in this section. Computers are employed widely as they are perfect for producing very flat floods of colour. Line drawings can be scanned into the computer and filled with colour, or the drawing can be originated on a computer (depending upon the drawing package), using very precise lines.

Full figure illustrations are not a necessity in this type of work. See *Drawing for Manufacture – Where to use a working drawing* and *Swimwear* examples in this section.

Swimwear/lingerie

When working in an area like lingerie or swimwear draw the full figure, encapsulating the pose, then concentrate on the torso for your actual design ideas. Good, shapely poses are required here to make the most of your designs (see *Women's, Men's and Children's poses* in *Drawing from Life*). Presentation will also play an important part and it can help to show the illustrations in some sort of stylised situation. Be careful not to overdo this, however, in case the illustration is overwhelmed. You need to collect visual information, that is, life drawing and photography, from different points of view so that you are fully informed about the proportions of the subject area.

A selection of poses has been provided to develop. It would make sense to illustrate using the profile or three-quarter view of the figure since this is where the pregnancy becomes most obvious. Front views of figures are not that helpful for illustrating maternity wear. However front, side and back views would need to be shown as 'working drawings' when the 'design' is being promoted See *Drawing for Manufacture*. Pregnancy in the very late stages obviously gives the most extreme silhouette for illustration and is the best for promoting maternity wear (as well as being the most crucial time for needing maternity wear!).

Select a template close to the shape of the garment required.

Trace the shape and illustrate stitching lines.

Add detail such as fastenings, stripings, etc.

Add more detail and include the placement of logos.

Illustrate logos and any requirements such as whether they are printed or embroidered or both.

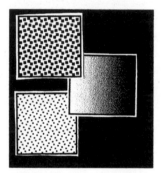

Add fabric textures, or prints and patterns.

Flood fill the design with fabric representation – flush with the outline.

Illustrate the back view concurrently with the front view.

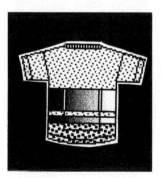

Here a back pocket is included.

For information on producing templates see *Drawing for Manufacture – Developing the template.*

The exercise on this page was executed using 'Claris Works' painting package and an Apple Macintosh Performa.

Ink the line on your pencil drawing using a technical drawing pen, 0.25, 0.35 or 0.5.

Select the appropriate marker pen colour and nib size (the broadest for flood filling your drawing).

Colour over your drawing and the edges smoothly.

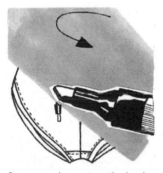

Reverse and repeat on the back if you require a slightly more intensified tone.

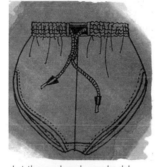

Let the marker dry and add more marker layers for great depth of colour.

When dry, cut out the drawing with a craft knife.

Remount on a contrasting background.

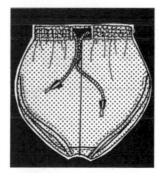

Tone (Letratone™) can be applied on its own, or over colour to add contrast.

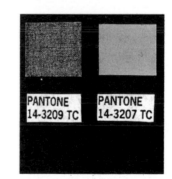

Pantone 'tria'™. marker pens come in a vast range of colours and are ideal for this type of work.

It is often required to produce coloured technical drawings for active sportswear; the colour needs to be applied very flat so that it does not overpower the detail.

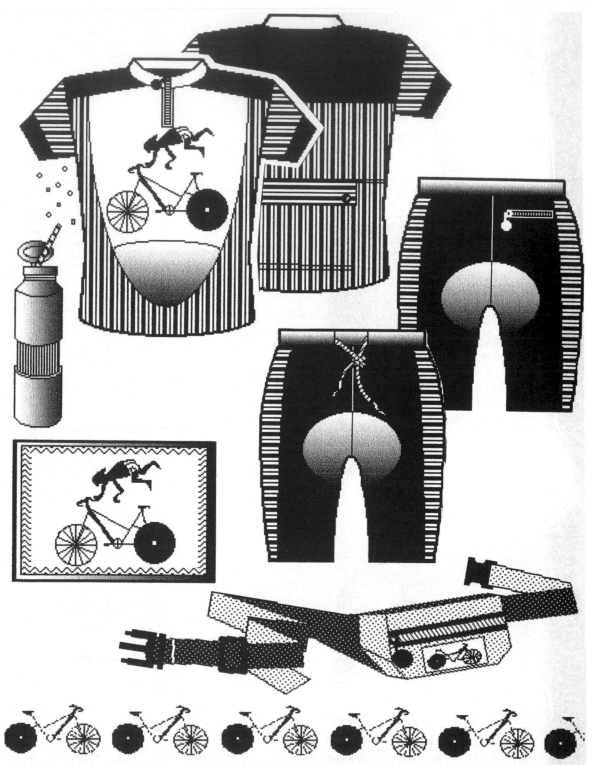

The example on this page was executed using 'Claris Works' painting package and an Apple Macintosh Performa.

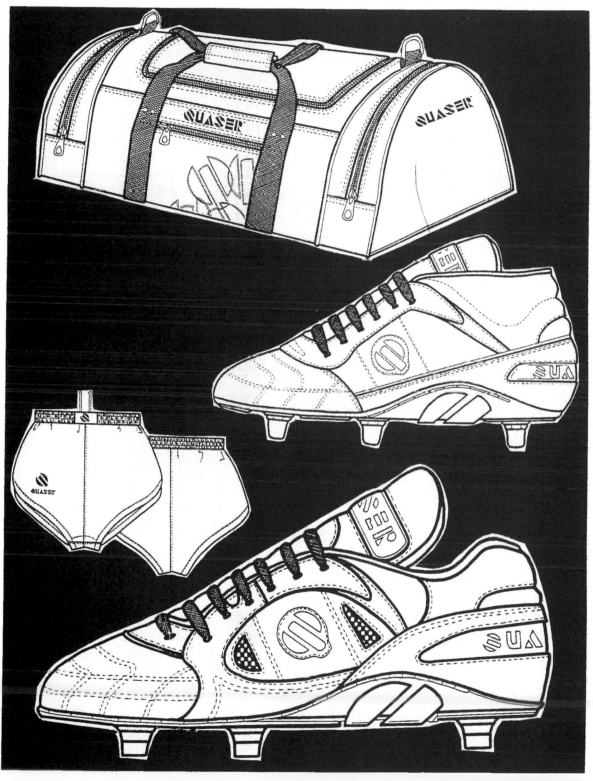

Example courtesy of Quaser Sports Limited. Note the great attention to detail and precise rendering of topstitching and logos.

Cropped figures, here, are confined to boxes but there is still room to communicate a lot of information. A variety of presentation techniques have been used to evoke an atmosphere for swimwear. The 'Sporty' illustrations of *swimwear* and *lingerie* were executed using a 'Claris Works' painting package and an Apple Macintosh Performa.

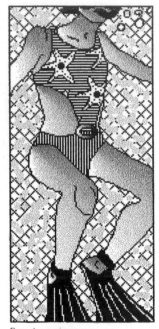

Sporty swimwear –
female child

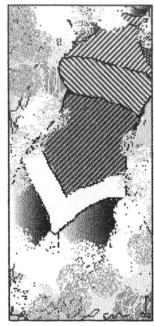

Sporty swimwear – woman

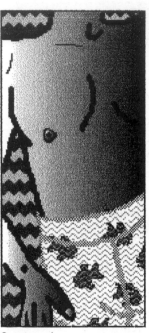

Sporty swimwear – man

Swimwear – female child

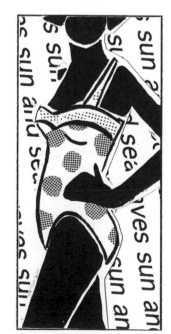

Swimwear – woman

Swimwear – man

The same approach has been applied as to *Swimwear*. Here the backgrounds are much simpler. Lingerie itself does not have as many 'themes' as swimwear to use as props, but the design research may provide more relevant backgrounds for presentation and so strengthen the illustration and consequently the promotion of the design.

Sporty lingerie – male child

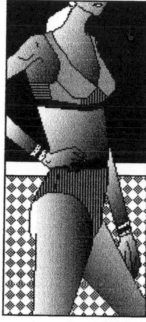

Sporty lingerie – woman

Sporty lingerie – man

Lingerie – female child

Lingerie – woman

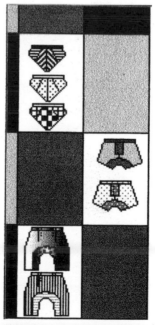

Lingerie – man

Cropping the pose for use in illustrating swimwear and lingerie. Refer to poses in *Drawing from Life*.

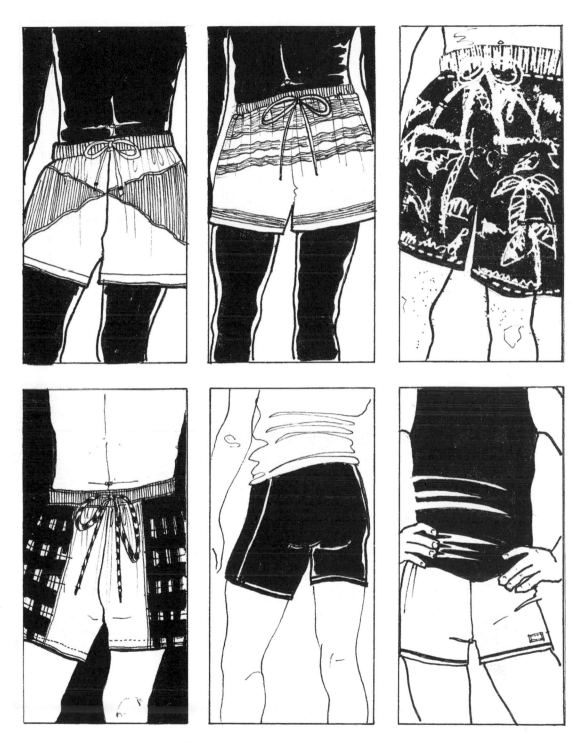

Men's swimwear using a variety of poses.

Accessories

Accessories may be designed/illustrated without figures, depending upon what is required. You may have to illustrate some figures. For example a rucksack can be very large, or very small, so it could be necessary to illustrate it on the body if exaggeration of scale was a key selling point. Alternatively you need carefully to illustrate a variety of rucksacks so that the difference of scale was made obvious – see the example of casual bags later in this section. You may find it easier to draw some of your own shoes, bags, hats, belts, etc. and then produce a shop report (see *Sketch Books – Shop or show reports*) of the area you are working on. This helps with research of design ideas, but also with contemporary ways of presenting your illustrations.

The method of approach provided in this section is that of using a pencil to make comparisons of measurement with your own accessories; for example, place a boot or shoe in front of you and use the pencil to plot height and length. When this is established, work out the relationship of construction lines with each other and only then work on the detail, always cross-referring one measurement to another.

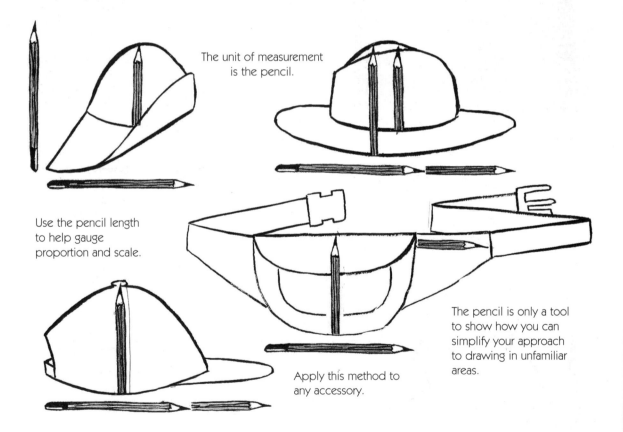

The unit of measurement is the pencil.

Use the pencil length to help gauge proportion and scale.

Apply this method to any accessory.

The pencil is only a tool to show how you can simplify your approach to drawing in unfamiliar areas.

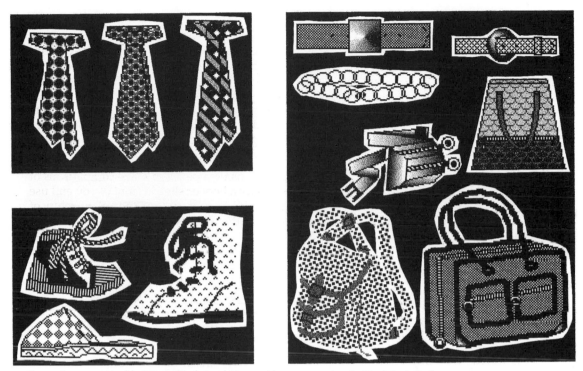

Examples generated in 'Claris Works' painting package on an Apple Macintosh Performa.
Note the lack of an outline on some drawings and the use of pattern mixes on others.

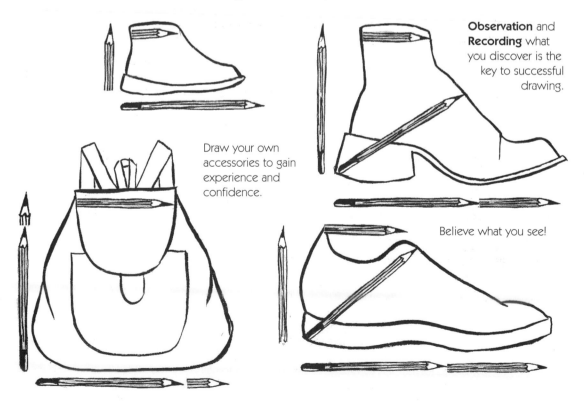

Observation and **Recording** what you discover is the key to successful drawing.

Draw your own accessories to gain experience and confidence.

Believe what you see!

Example courtesy of Jacqui Lee. This technique could be applied to gathering information for shop reports or as design development sheets with more technical information.

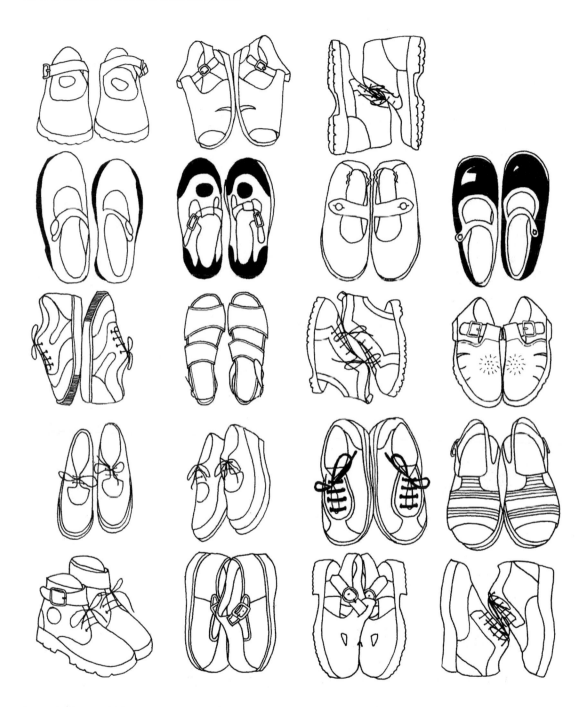

Example courtesy of Jacqui Lee. Note the clarity of line and alternative views of the shoes: for contrast – some are viewed from above, some from the side.

Example of casual bags courtesy of Jacqui Lee. Note the clarity of line and variety of scale. Pattern is used sparingly giving just enough contrast to the page.

Example courtesy of Janice Chadfield. Note the hand drawn detail contrasted with the photocopied texture/pattern collaged into the drawing. See *Media Techniques*.

AND FINALLY

The following is a *visual* checklist of the processes required during the illustrative life of a garment, with reference to the chapters in this book.

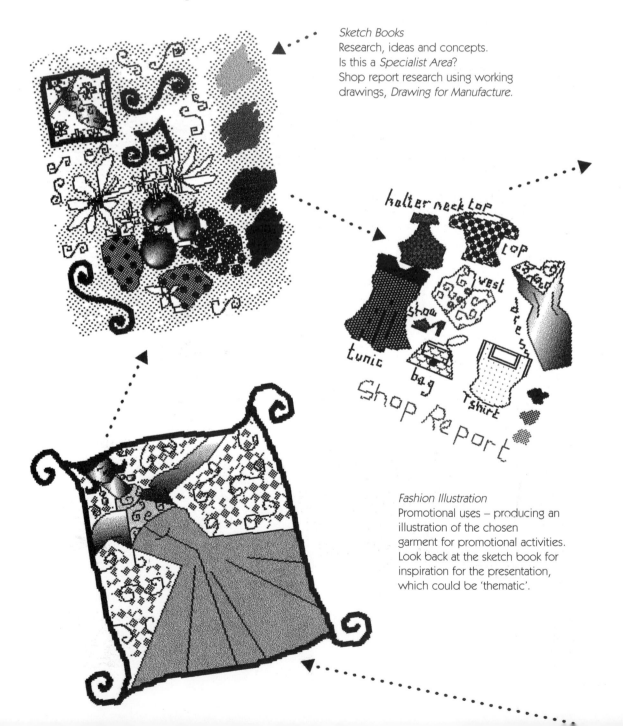

Sketch Books
Research, ideas and concepts.
Is this a *Specialist Area*?
Shop report research using working drawings, *Drawing for Manufacture*.

Fashion Illustration
Promotional uses – producing an illustration of the chosen garment for promotional activities. Look back at the sketch book for inspiration for the presentation, which could be 'thematic'.

The garment subject is a halter neck dress. It begins life as a sequence of ideas and concepts in the *Sketch Books*.

Fashion Illustration
Design development using
Media Techniques and
Fabric Representation.

Drawing from Life
Practising relevant poses.

Drawing for Manufacture
Choosing the garment to be
manufactured and producing a clear
working drawing with all details and
fabric swatches.

halter neck

detail

colour

silhouette

fabric print

Fashion Illustration
Illustrating the final range using
Media Techniques and
Fabric Representation.

Conclusion

The previous two pages are a visual guide to the uses of drawing in the life of a particular garment type, here a party dress. It is a simplistic way of understanding the different types of drawing that may be used within the industry. Of course this is not the only way to portray the many types of drawing but it should clarify what skills are needed where. Good figure drawing skills are desirable but working drawing skills are essential for the designer. Sketch book drawing is essential for the student and rapid drawing and observation is necessary for the gathering of research material. Exciting drawing is going to sell good ideas, but also sells mediocre ideas – ahead of someone who has good ideas but poor illustration skills.

This book has attempted to be as thorough as possible with its approach to fashion illustration at this time. Becoming competent at fashion illustration takes practise and an inquiring mind, although this book has given a variety of opportunities to speed up the process. Technology now plays its part and this is a great learning process in its own right. Not all areas of the industry are fully conversant, yet, with the versatility of the computer in illustration, but it is probably just a matter of time! However it must be reiterated that technology is not a substitute for real skill and good draughtsmanship is still the key to selling ideas successfully. Indeed, it is always going to be necessary to use some drawing to visualise personal ideas from the thought process to communicating them to others. Drawings are still, for the most part, scanned into the computer and then rendered, but we have shown some that are drawn directly on the screen when a scanner is not available. Hopefully this book will excite the reader to pursue the many different avenues currently open in fashion illustration.

One last, but certainly very important point must be about colour. The confines of this book only allow the reader to see illustration rendered in a variety of textures and tones of black. Initially this could have been seen as a drawback, but, in fact, it has been very useful in forcing us to put points across in a much more simplistic way. The use of colour has been referred to, but it is a whole other issue. Colour can be the most obvious attraction of an illustration and fashions in the use of colour are as important as those of drawing in a particular style or presenting work in a particular way. The use of many of the recipes included in *Media Techniques* can provide an infinite variety of effects from very slick to very naive work depending on the dictates of fashion. Personal interpretation will take on many different guises and colour is always helpful when working with design or prediction information.

The subject of illustrating fashion is a large and complex one but hopefully this book inspires the beginner or helps the experienced designer to improve their illustrative skills. All of the tools are here, the rest is up to you!

INDEX